T0348356

PERFECTED

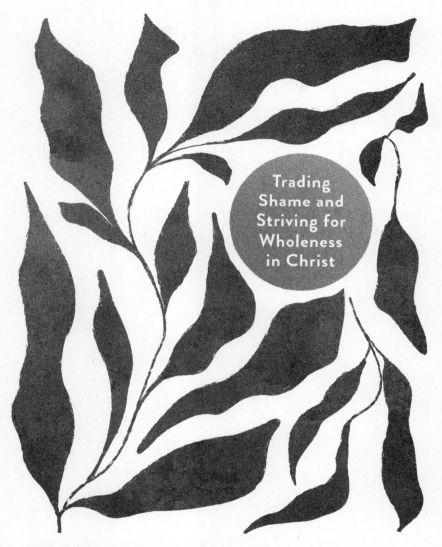

Trading Shame and Striving for Wholeness in Christ

PERFECTED

BETHANY BRODERICK

PUBLISHING®
BRENTWOOD, TENNESSEE

979-8-3845-0444-3

Published by B&H Publishing Group
Brentwood, Tennessee

Dewey Decimal Classification: 155.2
Subject Heading: PERFECTIONISM / SELF-
RELIANT LIVING / CHRISTIAN LIFE

Unless otherwise noted, all Scripture references
are taken from the Christian Standard Bible.
Copyright © 2017 by Holman Bible Publishers.
Used by permission. Christian Standard Bible®,
and CSB® are federally registered trademarks of
Holman Bible Publishers, all rights reserved.

Scripture references marked ESV are taken from the
Holy Bible, English Standard Version. ESV® Text
Edition: 2016. Copyright © 2001 by Crossway Bibles,
a publishing ministry of Good News Publishers.

Cover design by Lindy Kasler. Leaf image
by Palina Liashkovich/Stocksy. Watercolor
textures by white snow and Fandorina Liza/
Shutterstock. Author photo by Carmen Morris.

1 2 3 4 5 6 • 28 27 26 25

To Papa and CeeCee,
Thank you for your legacy as faithful grandparents,
authors, and most important, servants of Christ.

Acknowledgments

To my agent Dan, my editor Mary, and the rest of the team at B&H Publishing, thank you for taking a chance on a new author and guiding me every step of the way. Your insight and feedback made this book better than I could have ever hoped. Thank you for your belief in me and the message of this book.

To Ann and our Writing with Grace Mastermind group, I never would have made it this far without your expertise, your edits, and most important, your encouragement. You all have pushed me to love Christ more through my writing, and I wouldn't be the writer I am today without our group. It is a joy to walk this writing journey alongside each of you.

To the wonderful women at Exhale Creativity: Ashlee, who is the loudest cheerleader and most avid glitter thrower; Sarah, who was so generous to give feedback and to open doors; Sonya and Callie who first helped me realize there was a book inside me and gave me feedback on very early (and quite awful) drafts of the first chapter; and to the many other writers who I now have the privilege to call friends, thank you for creating a safe place for me to learn and grow as a writer.

To my dear friends who read rough drafts along the way: Eileen, Rachael, Amanda, Michelle, Neidy, Anna Clair, and Tara, thank you for your wise feedback and unending encouragement. I could not have gotten through the most difficult days of writing this book without motivating Marco Polo messages from Eileen and texts (with gifs) from Rachael. Your fingerprints are all over this book. Thank you, Staci, for your mentorship and support—and for making sure I didn't accidently write heresy.

To the local churches that have nurtured and equipped our family. This book is the fruit of seeds planted and watered by faithful sisters and brothers in Christ.

To Papa, my favorite editor, who read every single word of this book multiple times; to my family who has supported me and cheered for me every step of the journey: Dad, Myrissa, Laralyn, and CeeCee; and the biggest thanks to my mom, without whom this book would have never been written. From my earliest memory, you have always encouraged my love for writing and for Jesus. You watched my kids for countless hours while I scribbled on note cards, typed out words, and edited for the millionth time. You were always there to pray for me, to help me work out a chapter, and to remind me of truth when I felt anxious. I'm incredibly thankful to have a family who loves me and loves Jesus. I love you all!

To my sweet kiddos: Karis, Elias, and Anaya, you are my most precious treasures. Thank you for your grace while I learned to live out these truths as your mother. I pray what I have written in this book will overflow into our home. I love you!

To my husband Joseph, who, after listening to me talk about the book I wish I could read, asked me, "Why don't you just write the book?" Even though I grumbled back that one does not simply "just" write a book, your confidence in me helped me to move forward in obedience to God's call on my life. You have been a constant source of strength and wisdom as I prepared my proposal, anxiously sent (and waited on) emails, and spent hours at my desk writing and editing this book. You always believed in me (and what God was doing in me), even when I started to doubt. I love you, Babe; and thank you for being on my team.

Above all, I thank God, who started this good work in me and who will faithfully carry it to completion. Thank you, Jesus, for the rock-solid truth on which I can stand (and write): you have perfected me for all time.

Contents

Introduction

Am I good enough?

This question has plagued my heart and mind in every stage of life. As a child, I followed all the rules, memorized the assigned Bible verses, and sang the loudest in the children's choir—hoping for the nodding approval from my parents and teachers. As a teenager, I led youth group Bible studies, strove for straight A's in school, and counted every calorie entering my mouth out of a deep ache for my peers' acceptance and admiration. As a college student, I pushed through late hours of the night, perfecting a research paper as if my professor's rubric determined my identity. As a newlywed, I made spreadsheets with meal plans and cleaning schedules to be affirmed as a "good Christian wife." As a working woman, I labored over projects long past my paid hours because I felt burdened to prove my worth at my job. As a new mother, I imitated Instagram influencers, feeling like I would never live up to the standards in each tiny square. No matter how much I did, it never seemed to be *enough*.

Maybe you picked up this book because you, too, have felt this way. Perhaps you feel shame because you don't meet the expectations from those around you, from the voice inside your own head, or from Scripture. You may have strived to work hard, set goals, and discipline yourself, yet you feel like your efforts are still left wanting. When you fall into bed exhausted each night, your mind replays moments from the day like a broken record. You ask yourself: *Was I enough?*

The world tries to answer our self-doubt with glowing affirmations: *You've got this, girl! Just believe in yourself, and you can do it all! You are more than enough, just the way you are!* Even in the church, our struggles with identity are met with true—yet incomplete—promises: *God created you just as you are! You're a beautiful princess! You are enough in his eyes!* Still, all these phrases are merely bandages covering the festering wound of how inadequate we feel. These empty encouragements can never make us feel whole.

So how can we truly know if we are good enough?

What Is Enough?

The world often defines whether we are good enough by our level of education, our financial security, our social media following, or our clothing size. Yet the root of whether we feel good enough goes deeper than outward measures of success.

Merriam-Webster defines *enough* as "a degree or quantity that satisfies or that is sufficient."[1]

While Scripture doesn't give us a clear definition of the word *enough* as we would use it today, it does provide guidance on where our satisfaction and sufficiency should come from as believers. For example, when writing of his own qualifications as a minister of Christ, Paul describes what makes him confident that he is "enough:"

> Such is the confidence that we have through Christ toward God. Not that we are sufficient in ourselves to claim anything as coming from us, but our sufficiency is from God, who has made us sufficient to be ministers of a new covenant, not of the letter but of the Spirit. For the letter kills, but the Spirit gives life. (2 Cor. 3:4–6 ESV)

Paul could have boasted of his spiritual, cultural, and ethnic pedigree to prove his authority to the church in Corinth.[2] Before he met Christ, Paul was an elite Jew. He followed all the Jewish laws, studied under the right leaders, and worked hard to achieve authority in Jewish culture. He lived according to

---

1. *Merriam-Webster*, s.v. "enough," https://www.merriam-webster.com/dictionary/enough.
2. Philippians 3:4–6

the letter of the law to achieve religious perfection on his own. Yet he found those endeavors were futile—even life-killing. His zeal for man's approval had even led him to persecute those who followed Christ.

It was only when Paul beheld Christ on the road to Damascus that Paul realized his works would never be enough. When "a light from heaven suddenly flashed around him" (Acts 9:3), it exposed all the hidden darkness within him. Though physically blinded, Paul finally saw the depth of his sinfulness, the perfection of Christ, and the hope of the gospel.

Paul, at last, was free from his self-sufficient striving and self-condemning shame. "Everything that was a gain to me, I have considered to be a loss because of Christ" (Phil. 3:7). Surrendering his own prideful efforts and identity, Paul wanted to "be found in [Christ], not having a righteousness of my own from the law, but one that is through faith in Christ" (v. 9). He could now boast joyfully, not in himself, but in the sufficient goodness of Christ.

Releasing Our Shame and Striving

I resonate with Paul's life before meeting Christ, zealously pursuing the right things that would make me good enough for my family, my peers, myself, and even God. However, when I defined whether I was "good enough" by my spiritual disciplines, my emotional state, my children's behavior, and my career achievements, I was left empty. Centering my identity on my own ability to make myself perfect—to fulfill the letter of God's law—as Paul wrote, "killed" me.[3] I realized I could never make myself whole.

In this book, I share how God, in his grace and kindness, broke through the darkness of my heart. He shone a light on the sin I had tried to keep hidden for so long, but he also revealed the glory of his steadfast love for me. When I stopped trying to earn my own goodness by completing another Bible reading plan, committing to another volunteer opportunity at church, and achieving another career goal, I finally experienced his gift of abundant life. With Paul, I could count all my self-righteous works and shameful mistakes "to be a loss in view of the surpassing value of knowing Christ Jesus my Lord" (Phil. 3:8).

When I at last released my shame and striving, I could finally experience the freedom found in Christ's satisfaction and sufficiency. And, friend, if God could put together the broken pieces of my life into something whole, I know that he can do the same for you.

Finding Wholeness in Christ

I often have a nagging feeling in my gut that something is not quite right. Sometimes my stomach turns over insignificant

---

3. 2 Corinthians 3:6

worries: *Did I reschedule that doctor appointment? Did I turn off the oven before I left the house? Will I have time today to finish everything on my list?* Other times, my body roils with weightier doubts: *Am I doing a good job as a mother? Did I pass up an opportunity to share the gospel with my neighbor? What if I've missed God's call on my life?*

These anxieties—big and small—add up, often paralyzing me from moving forward. I'm so afraid that I've made a mistake, that I've missed something, that I haven't done enough, and I forfeit the promised peace of Christ. I wrongly believe that the solution to this constant white noise of anxiety is to try harder to be perfect on my own or to cover up my imperfections. I make more lists, plan carefully, and pray that my meager efforts are enough. Yet I know I'll always be found lacking.

Jesus offers something better than white-knuckled perfectionism. He promises that "he has perfected forever those who are sanctified" (Heb. 10:14). Friend, if you are in Christ, he has already *perfected you forever.* This perfection is more than a 4.0 GPA, an impeccable résumé, a tidy home, or a flawless appearance. It's not just an external ideal but an internal peace.

The Greek word translated "perfected" in this verse means "to make complete," or more specifically, "to add what is yet wanting in order to render a thing full."[4] Christ sees where you

---

4. Strong's, "teleioō," Blue Letter Bible, *Strong's Greek Lexicon (KJV)*, accessed March 16, 2024, https://www.blueletterbible.org/lexicon/g5048/kjv/tr/0-1/.

are lacking. He knows each imperfection you try to hide behind your shame and striving. He sees your every hidden sin, doubt, and weakness. But rather than heaping on more judgment and expectations, by *his* perfect sacrifice, Christ makes *you* "perfect and complete, lacking in nothing" (James 1:4 ESV). His perfected work in you frees you from anxious striving and fearful shame.

We are enough because he has made us enough. Christ Jesus has graciously filled us with his fullness[5] so that we may be *whole in him.*

How, then, when you are filled with anxiety about your worthiness and wholeness, can you fight the lies that tell you you're not enough with the truth that Christ has *perfected* you?

Fighting the Lies with Truth

Every time I share my testimony of struggling with shame, anxiety, perfectionism, legalism, and more, I hear a resounding echo of "me too." I'm encouraged to know I'm not the only one who wonders if she's enough. However, I'm also grieved because I'm not the only one Satan has deceived into a false sense of shame and striving.

How has our culture's emphasis on self-improvement manifested as legalism within the church? How has the

---

5. John 1:16

often-celebrated personality trait of perfectionism evolved into works-based righteousness? How have we become so focused on personal goodness that we've missed out on the goodness of God? Why do we cling to our shame as if we are people without hope? I hope to answer these questions, and more, in this book, so that you and I can, "demolish arguments and every proud thing that is raised up against the knowledge of God, [as] we take every thought captive to obey Christ" (2 Cor. 10:4–5).

Maybe you're like me, and you've pursued a self-righteous religious résumé yet have never felt good enough for God. Or maybe you're burdened with self-condemnation over the weight of your past sins, wondering how you could ever be good enough moving forward. I've been there too, friend. Neither way can make you feel whole. This book has good news for both the self-condemning and the self-righteous. It's my story, and probably some of your story. But mostly, it's the story of how Christ frees us from our shame and striving. It's the story of how Christ took our imperfections and perfected us. It's the story of how he can make us whole in him.

The question that will truly liberate us is not whether we are enough, but whether we believe that *Christ* is enough.

Walking Freely in Christ's Perfection

I pray as you read this book, we can together name Satan's lies that have held us captive, fight those lies with the truth of

God's Word, and walk freely in God's promises. I hope we can release our own striving for goodness and our shame that we are not good enough, and instead, we will hold fast to the perfect goodness of Christ.

Throughout this book, I'll use parts of my story along with the pastoral exhortations from Hebrews 10 to guide our journey to find our wholeness in Christ. In part 1, we'll dig up the root of the problem: putting obedience of God's law above enjoyment of God's love. We'll consider how our "do-it-yourself" culture has led to widespread "self-made religion" in the modern church (Col. 2:23).

In part 2, we will renew our minds with the biblical truth about God, ourselves, and our salvation. We'll expose the falsehoods in our view of God and learn how he's revealed himself as compassionate and gracious, slow to anger, and abounding in faithful love. We'll explore how God made us: created in his good image, with good limits, and called to good work. Then, we'll rejoice in Christ's work in us: how he has perfected us, is perfecting us, and will make us perfect forever.

Finally, in part 3, we'll discover the glorious promises of resting in Christ's finished work on our behalf: assurance of faith, enduring hope, love-motivated good works, and biblical community. At the end of each chapter, I'll offer you a "better affirmation"—a solid truth from God's Word to which you can cling rather than the empty encouragements of this world. I'll also include some reflection questions and journaling prompts to help you process what God may be teaching you through this book.

Today, if you feel heavy-laden by your vain efforts for sufficiency and satisfaction, I invite you to surrender your burdens at the foot of the cross. Lay down your guilt for all the imperfections and sins that weigh you down. We can bring our weary hearts to our good, gentle, and lowly Savior, "for [his] yoke is easy and [his] burden is light" (Matt. 11:30). Only when we take his yoke upon us will we find rest for our souls.

Only when we release our shame and our striving can we enjoy wholeness in Christ.

The
Lies

PART I

Chapter 1

Law over Love

He's going to find out I'm a fraud, I dreaded, clutching my closed Bible with clammy hands.

I wiped my palms across my pristine duvet cover. With gold, chocolate, and robin-blue stripes, it matched the rest of our "perfect" (albeit small) newlywed apartment. For the entirety of our thirteen-month engagement, I had curated our wedding registry along with my identity as a good Christian wife. Yet now my own imperfections marred my idealized expectations of marriage.

What will he think of me? I wept quietly, hoping not to alert my husband to my distress from the other room. *Will he think he married an unbeliever?*

We'd had another argument—this time about baked ziti, of all things. Anything could set off my fiery anger, leaving ashes all around me after my words spewed forth. There was the time he accidentally nicked me with a tool when he was unclogging my red hair out of the vacuum cleaner. And the time he flooded our kitchen while repairing the garbage disposal I had broken with too much leftover rice. This time, he had forgotten to put my premade casserole into the oven, and I arrived home late from my job hungry and furious. Even his smallest of missteps would unleash my furious criticism. I had known marriage would be hard to hold together—I hadn't realized it would be my own sins that would cause the first crack.

Living a "good" Christian life had been easier when I was a teenager, where I could hide my imperfections (particularly my temper and tongue) behind a closed door and purple-beaded curtain. Or when I lived in my college dorm room, where I could close myself in the bathroom when things got too difficult.

Now, though, I had nowhere to go. My hideous sins—the anger, the selfishness, the bitterness—that I had painstakingly covered for almost two decades were now on full display in the early days of my marriage. I had worried before about what he would think of my morning breath and tangled bedhead. Now, he had a front-row seat to my hot temper, my harsh words, and my lack of grace.

I glanced at the gold picture frame on my dresser holding our wedding photo. Our wedding was perfect. I looked perfect. Yet, it seemed like a lifetime ago, rather than only a year.

"Lord," I prayed aloud, "I'm sor . . ." A sob caught in my throat. "I'm so, so sorry. I haven't been a good Christian lately or a good wife or a good employee." Tears ran along the worn leather cover of my Bible.

I wasn't just broken over a single argument or the greater impact my anger was having on our marriage. The shame I had suppressed for much of my Christian life overwhelmed me. The pretense of perfection I had diligently maintained was falling apart before my eyes.

"I haven't been good at anything, but I promise I'm trying," I pleaded with the heavenly Father who seemed so distant to me. "I promise I'll do better tomorrow." Yet I knew I wouldn't be able to live up to the crushing expectations for goodness I perceived from God and, even more so, from the church.

My Religious Pedigree

I grew up in a home and church that thoroughly loved me, the Lord, and the gospel. My family, teachers, and countless mentors poured biblical knowledge into my heart and mind during those formative years. I attended church three times a week (sometimes more with my minister father) and was educated in a Christian school. I read all the popular religious books for teens. I went on every summer mission trip—from my backyard to the Middle East—and every winter youth retreat. Like Paul,[1] I felt I had achieved the utmost religious pedigree.

Still, doubts and questions plagued my spirit: *Did God really mean it when he said his grace is sufficient? Why would God include*

---

1. Philippians 3:4–6

all those rules if good behavior wasn't what he valued most? Don't you need to make yourself worthy to receive his love? You know that only the good girls get the good life. What would God think of you if you made a mistake—what would your parents and church think of you? How can you ever be good enough?

I wouldn't realize it until later in my life, but Satan used my biblical knowledge against me. He twisted the Word of God that had been planted in my heart. Throughout my spiritual journey, he whispered the same question he used to seduce Eve: "Did God really say . . . ?" (Gen. 3:1).

I bit the fruit of Satan's trap. I strived to be that good girl because I believed that God's love for me depended on my ability to perform for him. I believed that the church's acceptance of me relied on my own righteous works. I wanted to fit in perfectly to the lofty standards of cultural Christianity and, based on the outward appearances, it looked like I had succeeded. I submitted to my parents, made good grades, dated the right boys, got into college, and stayed involved in church. I had it all together, yet I still held God—and most others—at arm's distance. I feared if they got too close, they would see through the "perfect" mirage I had created.

While I may have looked like I had it all together on the outside, I knew the deep darkness of my heart. I was all too aware of the lustful thoughts festering in my mind, the angry words waiting on the tip of my tongue, and the critical spirit brewing in my heart. Yet I could never confess these sins in fear that I would lose my spot on the pedestal. Rather than experience God's gracious forgiveness for my sins, I remained burdened by the shame of my (poorly) hidden imperfections, and I strove even harder for perfection.

Guilt over Gratitude

While at times I've felt isolated in my shame and striving, I know I'm not the only follower of Christ who has fallen for the same deception. Maybe you, too, have fallen for Western culture's ideals of self-improvement and self-sufficiency that have seeped into Christian churches in the form of legalism. We can focus more on checking off our Bible reading plans than being changed by the Word of God. We set goals to be more generous, to share the gospel more, and to pray for our church missionaries—often striving in our own effort rather than relying on the Spirit's work within us. We may appear to do all the right things on the outside, but on the inside, we are dying in our self-sufficient search for goodness. Phylicia Masonheimer defines these legalistic mentalities "as trying to take a shortcut to holiness."[2] It's using the law to elevate oneself rather than to draw closer to God.

---

2. Phylicia Masonheimer, *Verity*, podcast audio, November 17, 2022, https://veritybyphylicia.libsyn.com/088-how-to-find-freedom-from-legalism.

While most Christians aren't legalistic to the point of truly believing their works will save them, Daniel Doriani points out that believers can easily fall into lesser "classes" of legalism. He writes: "Class-four legalists . . . so accentuate obedience to the law of God that other ideas shrivel up. They reason, 'God has redeemed us at the cost of his Son's life. Now he demands our service in return.'"[3] Doriani argues that an entire sermon can be filled with truth yet still be oppressive, because it motivates Christians to obey out of guilt rather than gratitude.

In the faith context where I grew up, this definition of legalism looked like flannel-board Bible stories compelling us to live up to the faith giants of Abraham, David, and Daniel. It was proclaimed every Wednesday night in youth group when we were admonished not to commit one of the three "big" sins—sex, drugs, and alcohol. It was woven through Bible studies that promoted behavior modification over a relationship with God. By the time I reached young adulthood, I had so dwelt on the law of God that I had forgotten the love of God.

I knew a lot about how to be good, but not as much about the goodness of God.

---

3. Daniel M. Doriani, *Putting the Truth to Work: The Theory and Practice of Biblical Application* (Phillipsburg, NJ: P&R Publishing, 2001), 279.

Fig-Leaf Coverings

I began to despair in those early days of my marriage. I felt like Adam and Eve in the garden, finally acknowledging my shameful nakedness. As I tried hiding my dirty laundry from my husband, I also tried hiding myself from God—weaving together fig leaves of more Bible studies, more mournful apologies, and more good deeds to make up for my mistakes. While I knew both God and my husband must love me, I questioned how I could ever be worthy enough to deserve it.

Despite my paralyzing guilt, I returned every day to my perfectly made bed with my Bible, journal, and pen in hand. In my shame, I couldn't raise my eyes to heaven, yet I poured my words out onto the page:

> *Father, I have a horrible fear of failure. I'm afraid I'll fall short of my expectations, but especially others' expectations. That fear extends to you. I am so afraid of letting you down. When I've missed my quiet time for a few days. I am scared to come back because of my failure. Sometimes, I won't pray because I am worried you will only condemn me. I fear that I am not good enough.*

The cycle continued for weeks and then months. I would come before the Lord, pleading for him to forgive me of my sin, release me from the shame—all while promising to do better next time. While I believed in grace, I withheld it from myself until I felt like I deserved it. To assuage my guilt, I began saying a prayer for salvation each night, hoping that this time, something would "stick." Yet I never found any relief.

No Condemnation

One Sunday, my pastor held up a small book—*Stop Asking Jesus into Your Heart* by J. D. Greear—at the end of the sermon. He offered it for free to any visitor who was unsure if they were truly a follower of Christ and who would like to talk with him after the service. While I could have purchased a copy in the church lobby for a discounted rate, I didn't want anyone to suspect I had doubts and insecurities about my faith. Instead, I discreetly purchased the e-book on my Kindle when I got home. I prayed this would hold the key to finally feeling secure in my relationship with the Lord, or more important, finally being the perfect Christian woman I was raised to be.

That afternoon, I turned on my Kindle and tapped the neon-yellow cover image. Only a couple chapters in, God used Greear's words to pierce my guarded heart: "We may not be worthy to be forgiven, but He is worthy to forgive us."[4] I started to realize my overwhelming shame did not come from the Holy Spirit's conviction, but from Satan's deceit. My focus on

4. J. D. Greear, *Stop Asking Jesus into Your Heart: How to Know for Sure You Are Saved* (Nashville: B&H Publishing Group, 2013), 30.

my own biblical knowledge and religious performance had kept me from experiencing the freedom found in Christ's finished work. I felt my burden lift with each swipe of the page. At last, I could lift my eyes off my own imperfections and, instead, look to the perfection of Christ.

A footnote in the book prompted me to open my Bible for the first time in months. I flipped to Romans 8 and started reading: "Therefore, there is now no condemnation for those in Christ Jesus, because the law of the Spirit of life in Christ Jesus has set you free from the law of sin and death" (vv. 1–2).

I dropped my Bible into my lap and took a gulp of air, feeling like I could breathe at long last. For longer than I could remember, I had been trying to prove my own perfection before God. I had grown up believing God's greatest desire was for me to be good—to be the best example of his goodness to those around me. Now, I realized his greatest desire was for me to be *his*. I returned to my tear-stained journal:

> *Father, lately I have been pouring self-condemnation on myself—for sinning, for not spending time with you, for not evangelizing—and it has crippled my relationship with you. I come to my quiet time feeling guilty, and I spend most of (if not all) the time trying to plead for your forgiveness when you have already poured your love on me. I have been living in defeat, believing the deceiver's lies that you didn't*

*mean it when you covered my sins. I have hidden
from you, faking a spiritual exterior to others. I cannot do this.*

*But you don't need me to do anything. You
have already done everything. You have chosen me.
You sent your Son as the perfect sacrifice for my
sin. You graciously poured out your wrath on him
so that we do not have to feel condemnation. You
love me. You do not require perfection, for I am
already covered with Christ's perfection.*

Your grace is enough for me.

While I tasted freedom for the first time that night, I didn't
want to share the experience with anyone, even my husband.
While I knew Christ covered all my imperfections, I still felt
the weight of the expectations of those around me. I thought
I must be the only one who struggled this way—the only one
burdened by shame and striving.

In the years that followed, I would learn how many other
brothers and sisters in Christ are held captive by these same lies.

You've Got This

Western culture often proclaims we can attain any dream,
any goal, and any achievement with our own hard work. They
tell us: *You got this. You're enough. If you just dream big enough*

and work hard enough, you can be anything you want to be. The only thing that is standing in your way is you.

While those sentiments are all motivating, they're lies (or half-truths at best). Yet we apply those same worldly affirmations to our spiritual life. Our faith becomes just one more aspect of our dream life that can be achieved with a lot of elbow grease and a little prayer. We proudly check off day after day in a Bible reading plan without slowing down long enough to hear what God has to say. We commit to more volunteer requests at church in hopes of receiving recognition and appreciation from church leaders. We fill our Amazon shopping cart with more Christian resources, believing more of the "right" stuff will help us become who we hope to be.

However, these kinds of positive affirmations are useless unless they are grounded in something true. Deep down— beneath all the biblical knowledge, rule-following, and church service—we often sense we can't truly be good enough on our own. While God has indeed called his people to a life of increasing holiness,[5] our white-knuckled efforts often drive us deeper into self-sufficiency or self-condemnation rather into the wholeness found in our holy God.

Instead of freeing us to be who God created us to be, these affirmations of inner goodness weigh us down with expectations

---

5. 1 Peter 1:15

that we can never fulfill in our own strength. We are being told every day to pick ourselves up by our own bootstraps and accomplish our American Christian dream—trying to secure for ourselves the promises of peace, joy, and success found in God's Word. Yet as Gloria Furman wrote: "The bootstraps of self-righteousness are chains."[6]

Rather than submit to our gentle and lowly Savior and take on his easy yoke,[7] we groan under the heavy load of our own making, whispering to ourselves, "I've got this." Yet when we fix our eyes on our own righteousness, we become trapped in a prideful cycle of shame and striving.

Two Faces of Pride

When life was relatively easy—especially in my high school and college years—I bought into those self-sufficient affirmations and could maintain the façade of perfection. I worked hard to jump through all the religious hoops and prove my Christian worth to God, my parents, and anyone who would grant me their approval. I led my school's prayer ministry, wrote devotionals for my small group, and volunteered with my church after a natural disaster struck our community. At the same time, I was boastful and arrogant—looking down in self-righteous

6. Gloria Furman, *The Pastor's Wife: Strengthened by Grace for a Life of Love* (Wheaton, IL: Crossway, 2015), 31.
7. Matthew 11:29–30

judgment on other believers who more visibly struggled with sin, doubt, and hardship. I pridefully assumed credit for my own Christian "success."

During harder seasons of my life—like at the beginning of my marriage—those empowering platitudes rung hollow. No amount of self-care and self-talk could relieve the burden of my inevitable failure. I heaped shame upon myself until I felt I'd paid the penance for my imperfections. I pridefully rejected grace—judging myself just as harshly (if not more) as I had judged others.

I've repeated this cycle more times than I can count—swinging back and forth between self-righteousness and self-condemnation. Now I've learned that both shame and striving are two sides of the same coin of pride.[8] Self-righteousness is false confidence. It idolizes our own ability to follow rules, reach goals, and be good. Self-condemnation is false humility. While it may appear to be the better of the two options, it still fixes our eyes on ourselves, with all our failures and weaknesses.

Neither striving nor shame lift our eyes to Jesus. Neither reflect the true gospel of grace.

---

8. Timothy Keller, *The Freedom of Self-Forgetfulness* (Leyland, England: 10Publishing, 2012).

The Extravagant Father

In Luke 15, Jesus told the story of a good father who had two sons. The younger son was impetuous and lustful. He selfishly demanded his inheritance from his father, as if wishing his father were dead, but squandered it away in a life of "reckless living" (v. 13 ESV). He eventually became destitute to the point of eating discarded pig food. Ashamed, he began walking toward his father's house, hoping that he could be welcomed back as a lowly servant.

"But while the son was still a long way off, his father saw him and was filled with compassion. He ran, threw his arms around his neck, and kissed him" (v. 20). Running was one of the most shameful acts for a Middle Eastern man in that culture, yet the father humiliated himself so he could set his son free from his own shame.[9] He welcomed his son back home with open arms and threw a grand feast in his honor.

The older son had remained by the father's side during his brother's rebellion. He strove to honor his father, learn their trade, and obey the rules. Yet he did not do so out of love for his father, but from a selfish desire for reward and recognition. The older brother may have appeared faithful, but he was just as self-centered as his younger brother. When he saw his wasteful

---

9. Kristi McLelland, *Jesus and Women in the First Century and Now* (Nashville: Lifeway Press, 2019).

brother being celebrated with a fattened calf, the older brother lashed out in anger toward his father. He believed his brother was receiving better treatment than he had received.

Again, in his extravagant love, the father sought out his prideful son and entreated him to enjoy the celebration: "Son, . . . you are always with me, and everything I have is yours" (v. 31). The father reminded his eldest son that while the younger brother starved with the pigs, he had freely enjoyed the abundance of the father. All the father's blessings were freely available to him as well, whether or not he fulfilled the cultural expectation of being a good son.

While this parable is often titled "The Prodigal Son" in our English translations, Jesus focused his story not on the two wayward sons but on the forgiving father. The narrative does not center on the excessive guilt of the younger brother or the unbridled pride of the older. Rather, it tells the story of the father's extravagant grace. It was the father who chased after the younger son who hung his head in self-condemnation. It was the father who beckoned the older son held captive by his self-righteousness.

Just as both sons needed to be reminded of the goodness of their father, our heavenly Father rescued us from the bondage of our sinful pride—whether it manifests as self-condemnation or self-righteousness. While I have played the role of both brothers in my life, it's the older brother with whom I more often resonate.

27

He did all the right things and was still woefully unhappy. He spent his life trying to prove his worth to his father, yet he still felt empty. In his vain efforts, the older brother missed the love and acceptance his father freely offered him.

I have spent much of my Christian life striving in self-righteousness instead of resting in the righteousness of the perfect Son, Jesus Christ—"the pioneer and perfecter of our faith" (Heb. 12:2). Years of bitterness and anger passed before I realized that I was welcomed into the Father's house just as I am. But despite the lavish love and forgiveness available to us, many believers, like me, still hang our heads in shame and strain ahead in striving.

Perfected Once for All

We aren't the first generation of believers Satan has weighed down with shame and striving. The same legalistic struggles pervaded the early church, especially the audience of the book of Hebrews. The unknown author wrote this rich sermon to a congregation of Jewish Christians a few decades after the death of Christ. Emperor Nero was ramping up persecution of Christians in the Roman Empire, and these young believers struggled to find their place when they were rejected by both religious Jewish culture and the secular Roman culture. Taking advantage of this pressure, Satan began tempting them to look back to rituals and rules of Judaism that appeared safer and more controllable than the sacrifice and surrender of Christianity.

In the first nine chapters, the author of Hebrews knocks down the pillars of this gospel of works one after another. No angel can provide better revelation of God than Jesus. No spiritual leader like Moses or Abraham could keep the law of God better than Jesus. No priest, sacrifice, or temple could bring them into the loving presence of God than the better perfect priest, sacrifice, and temple of Jesus. Jesus is better than anything we could ever offer him—better than anything we can do to make ourselves whole.

The Spirit-inspired words of the author knock down pillars in my own life as well. The belief that God withholds his approval and blessings when I fail. The pressure to prove myself to God and those around me. The prideful self-sufficiency that refuses to turn to the gracious Father, the compassionate Savior, and the comforting Holy Spirit.

In the tenth chapter of Hebrews, the author narrows in on one of the biggest strongholds in the lives of these believers. He addresses the sacrificial system which had been in place since God delivered his people out of Egypt. In this chapter, the author attempts to set right the balance between God's law and God's love. The writer of Hebrews wants the church—both then and now—to rest in the perfect work Christ accomplished for us on the cross. We no longer bear the weight of making ourselves good enough before God because "he has *perfected forever* those who are sanctified" (Heb. 10:14, emphasis added).

Hebrews 10 relieves us of the burden of self-righteous works, declaring it impossible for our own good deeds to take away our sin.[10] Yet it also gives hope to those trapped in self-condemnation, reminding us we have confidence to enter the presence of God by the blood of Christ.[11] So whether we feel pride or shame in how good we are today, Hebrews 10 beckons us to trade our shame and striving for wholeness in Christ.

The Law Never Satisfies

Despite that pivotal moment in my bedroom years ago, I still struggle to rest in God's love for me rather than my own work for him. It's easier to fall back into my old habits of obeying the law in my own strength rather than relying on his Spirit to work in me. I'm tempted to focus on my adherence to rules rather than my relationship with God.

I must daily remind myself of the law's place in God's redemptive story. The law reveals God's holiness and humanity's sinfulness, and it points us to the hope of a perfect Savior. But adherence to the law could never bring life.[12] Only through the life, death, and resurrection of Christ could we at last be

---

10. Hebrews 10:4
11. Hebrews 10:19
12. Galatians 3:19–22

made children of God.[13] "Love consists in this: not that we loved God, but that he loved us and sent his Son to be the atoning sacrifice for our sins" (1 John 4:10). Our faith is not in God's law but in his love.

Obeying the law will never satisfy us like the love of Christ can. No amount of good works can ever make us feel enough like resting in the good work Christ has done on our behalf. Rather than staying trapped in the cycle of self-righteousness and self-condemnation, we can lift our eyes to Christ who has perfected us and made us whole in him.

So whether you're more like the younger brother who squandered away his father's riches or the older brother who wasted the privilege of his father's presence, the heavenly Father will forever welcome you back to him. You can reject the lie that God wants your good behavior more than he wants you to run to him with your heart, broken and humble.[14]

And you and I can trust that, in his grace and love, God is always running toward us.

---

13. Galatians 3:26
14. Psalm 51:16–17

Remember

When you feel like God's affection for you is determined by your good work for him, you can trade your shame and striving for the truth that:

I am enough because God loves me unconditionally.

Reflect

1. Are you tempted to measure your worth by the good things you can accomplish? How has that affected your relationship with God?

2. In what areas of your life have you experienced self-condemnation? What would it look like for you to believe the truth that Christ does not condemn you?

3. Are you more like the older or younger brother in the story of the Prodigal Son? How have you experienced the heavenly Father "running" to you in love?

Read

For further study, read Romans 8:1–11. Think about areas of your life where you still feel shame. Write down a prayer based on these verses, thanking God that you are no longer condemned by him. Ask him to help you walk confidently in the freedom Christ has won for you.

Chapter 2
DIY Religion

I spent most Saturdays in my early twenties wandering the aisles of thrift stores. Hoping to find my next fixer-upper project, I sifted through stalls filled with dusty Coca-Cola bottles, tattered football memorabilia, and heaps of wood begging to be turned into shiplap. I ran my fingers along delicate lace, antique school desks, and even rusty basket bicycles—all costing more than they did in their prime. I wanted something vintage but not *so* vintage it would cost me an arm and a leg. I wanted something shabby but not *so* shabby that it would require me to learn how to use a sander.

The first treasure I squeezed into the trunk of my compact sedan was a set of worn, white shutters. I set them up against the shed in our backyard, hoping a can of teal spray paint would breathe new life into them. When I finished their restoration, I hung them on either side of the mirror in our tiny bathroom and clipped Bible verses onto the slats with clothespins. I could almost hear Joanna Gaines' approving drawl behind me.

On a shelf in our cramped laundry closet, I hoarded two dozen wine bottles to repurpose. One winter I burned off all my fingertips hot-gluing twine and buttons onto three of these spray-painted (also teal) glass bottles. I set the trio on my kitchen table as a centerpiece. The rest remained untouched until they were thrown away in a move.

My treasures piled up. Painted and distressed picture frames. Windowpanes given fresh purpose as chalkboards and mirrors. Old canvases mod-podged with new memories.

As adept as I was at painting over dingy wood, I was equally adept in painting my own life with the appearance of perfection. I filled in the cracks of imperfection with a stroke of white lies—blaming mistakes at work on computer errors, giving phony excuses to friends as to why I had forgotten our coffee date, and blaming my husband's poor listening skills to cover up what I had forgotten.

In our church small group, I mastered the art of offering prayer requests and appearing invested without ever revealing the doubts about my faith and appearing weak. I attended women's Bible study and recited the spiritual lingo necessary to feel accepted, sharing how I was "blessed" and where I needed "new morning mercies." I splashed cold water on my face before guests arrived at our house for weekly game nights—hoping they couldn't tell my husband and I had been arguing mere moments before they knocked.

As inner perfection became increasingly difficult to maintain, I endeavored to polish my exterior. I kept a fastidious running routine, checking off each day's activities on a paper calendar on my bedside table. I tracked calories on a phone app, afraid to weigh an ounce over my wedding weight. With our meager newlywed budget, I shopped at consignment stores in the nicer area of town, hoping to afford designer clothes to fit in with my coworkers.

Like the spray paint that covered the flaws on the shutters, I perfected my swipe of concealer to hide my puffy, red eyes from nights of crying myself to sleep. I was struggling in my faith and feeling the oppressive weight of expectations—from the world and from myself—yet I smiled through it all. If for a moment I let down my guard, I believed I would be discarded like the broken and battered pieces left unpurchased at the antique store.

Every morning, I ate breakfast at our table next to the wine bottles I had taken great pains to refurbish. Despite the elegance of the twine and lace exterior, I felt as empty as they were.

Do-It-Yourself Culture

I know I'm not alone in my struggle to maintain the façade of perfection. Our culture commands you and me to do it *all*, and to do it *ourselves*, and do it *better* than someone else. Media monetizes our impulse for improvement by creating an entire industry that helps us to "do-it-yourself" (DIY). There are shows, magazines, and social media accounts dedicated to promoting DIY methods for renovating a home, cooking a gourmet meal, and hosting a perfect party (or even watching people fall apart trying).

Unfortunately, this pressure to do everything perfectly isn't limited to secular culture. I'm often caught in the endless cycle of Instagram reels that teach me how to properly highlight my Bible, how to train my children in the Lord, and how to hold the "biblical" stance on any given issue. I feel pressure to imitate Christian influencers, writers, and celebrities (even godly ones). I share their posts, use their journals, and buy their beautiful art prints with curated verses, hoping to attain the ideal Christian life. A life where I do not struggle with a hot temper or gnawing doubts. One where I never miss a day of a Bible reading plan. One where I'm praised by my peers for my knowledge and insight.

While many of these resources are beneficial to my spiritual growth, I'm tempted to wrongly believe that if I can fill my life with enough of the right tools, I could manufacture the same Christian life I see portrayed on social media. If I just set goals and work hard, I will feel whole. I will be a "good Christian woman."

I create a "DIY religion" of sorts. Yet no matter how much I try to hold myself together, the cracks always break through.

How We Got Here

In her book *Enough about Me*, Jen Oshman traces how we arrived at this DIY, self-help culture.[1] Western culture has spent hundreds of years cultivating a worldview of individualism and relativism. Individualism tells us that we can be independent and self-reliant. Relativism tells us that we can make our own truth. The combination of the two is deadly to the Christian life.

This cultural worldview has led to the widespread message: "You can do it all!" Yet rather than free us, this command enslaves us. Oshman writes:

> To uphold this worldview, we must become our own masters. Ironically, we don't actually become free. We must not only muster our own meaning and goals and dreams, but we must supply our own energy and ability to accomplish them. . . . This makes us fragile. It's all on us. Today we have to create our worlds and make them go round too.[2]

I've felt this cultural trend even more acutely as a woman. Because we have more ways to work outside the home and more

---

1. Jen Oshman, *Enough about Me: Finding Lasting Joy in the Age of Self* (Wheaton, IL: Crossway, 2020).
2. Oshman, *Enough about Me*, 35.

resources for our work inside the home, we feel an increased pressure to do it all. While we have better opportunities and circumstances than generations before us, women are more unhappy than we have ever been.[3] While we may have been freed from some historical oppression, we are now oppressed by the expectations of how to "make the most" of our freedom.

The business executive puts in sixty hours to rise above her male colleagues at a successful company. The young mom stays up all night to create a balloon arch and bake a smash cake for her baby's first birthday (and to post it on Instagram). The college student sacrifices sleep to maintain a 4.0 GPA and pad her social calendar and résumé. We're exhausted, yet we can't stop because we know our meager efforts are still not enough.

We groan under the pressure of this DIY culture.

The Crushing Weight of Expectations

The buttery scent of popcorn filled the living room, as our family snuggled under fuzzy blankets for our weekly movie night. We scrolled through Disney+, finally choosing a new animated film that everyone seemed to be posting about on social media: *Encanto*.

---

3. Sherri Bourg Carter, "Meet the Least Happy People in America," *Psychology Today*, September 17, 2011, http://www.psychologytoday.com/us/blog/high-octane-women/201109/meet-the-least-happy-people-in-america.

After enduring tragedy, a Colombian family receives the gift of an enchanted house and magical talents they can use to rebuild their community. Feeling the burden to prove themselves worthy of this miracle, the family's matriarch, Abuela Madrigal, demands perfection from every family member. Mirabel—the central character and only family member without a gift—struggles to find how she can earn the approval of her Abuela and serve her community without the magic.

My children and I were delighted by the colorful characters and soundtrack. But as I continued to watch, the movie touched tender spots in my heart. While my children were enchanted by the catchy tune, "We Don't Talk about Bruno," I was gripped by the songs from Mirabel's older sisters. My chest tightened when Louisa sang of the pressure to carry everything and never break a sweat in "Surface Pressure." I knew how it felt to be crushed by the expectations of my family and community and to long for freedom to enjoy life and relax. My heart ached with Isabelle when she belted her hope to free herself from the need to be perfect in everything she did in "What Else Can I Do?" I, too, have wondered who I could be if I wasn't so concerned with pleasing everyone around me.

At the end of the film, Abuela Madrigal finally understood the unbearable expectations she had placed on her family, and she wrapped Mirabel in an accepting embrace. Tears flowed freely down my cheeks. "What's wrong, Mommy?" My three-year-old daughter was bewildered why a flock of golden butterflies and a hug would make me cry.

"I just really like this movie," is all I could reply.

While this may seem like a childish example (it's *just* a movie), the characters reveal the deeper longing of our culture. The movie resonated with adults and children alike (and won multiple awards) because our society is often like Abuela Madrigal. It's a demanding master who expects each and every person to contribute something extraordinary, something beautiful, or something perfect to society. If we can't meet our culture's standards, how can we be good enough?

Even within the church, believers can feel the expectations to put themselves together before showing up for service on Sunday morning. Instead of coming with our brokenness to be encouraged and edified by the body of Christ, we put on our best dress, a smile, and the pretense of perfection for a couple hours a week. We keep our brothers and sisters in Christ at a distance—either because we hope to hide our weaknesses or we believe we're stronger without them.

Why are we burdened by this weight to appear like we have it all together? Why do we have this longing for perfection?

Made for Perfection

In the first chapter of the Bible, God describes how he created humanity in his image.[4] He made man and woman to reflect his character—his holiness, goodness, righteousness, loving-kindness—and to continue his perfect work on earth. He designed humanity to live in a perfect garden, to labor in perfect harmony, and to walk in perfect communion with himself. Humanity still deeply longs to be perfect because we were created for perfection.

That perfect life wasn't enough for Adam and Eve, though. They believed the serpent's lie that they could live a better life outside of God's good design. So they ate the fruit, and for the first time, they realized their nakedness and shame. Their eyes were opened to imperfection, and they sought to cover up their flaws with fig leaves.

Since the day our first parents sinned, God's image in us has been marred by our selfish desires and ambitions. His perfect creation is torn apart by war and disaster. Perfect communion with God and others is hindered by hatred and pride. Our once-perfect bodies are wrecked by disease and addiction. Yet our imperfect world yearns to be fully redeemed. "Not only [creation], but we ourselves who have the Spirit as the

---

4. Genesis 1:27

firstfruits—we also groan within ourselves, eagerly waiting for adoption, the redemption of our bodies" (Rom. 8:23).

We groan over our imperfections—and with our attempts to conceal them—because our body, mind, and spirit were created for perfection. Our desire for perfection is a holy longing because God created us to reflect his perfection. The problem is not in our desire for wholeness, but in where we search for the fulfillment of our desire. We often look to this world or inside ourselves for answers rather than to our Creator.

Many of us attempt to repair our marred perfection like a DIY craft project. While we trust in Jesus for our salvation, we believe the rest of our Christian life is up to us. We live as if God's grace ends after Jesus paid for the punishment of our sins. While we may sing about the "Amazing Grace" that saved us, we're not living as if the same grace sustains us.

Missing Half the Gospel

To illustrate this point, I once heard a pastor[5] compare Christians who live like this to a man with great debt who walks into a bank and pleads for mercy. The magnanimous banker forgives all the man's debts and sends him out the door debt-free. Yet the man is still penniless. He will spend the rest of his life trying to earn money to make ends meet, praying he

---

5. Joby Martin, interview with Jamie Ivey, *The Happy Hour*, podcast audio, #487, "What the Empty Tomb Means for Us," April 20, 2022.

will not fall back into debt. This is an incomplete picture of the gospel we often believe.

The full gospel is like a man with great debt who walks into a bank, and the benevolent banker *adopts him as a son*. The banker pays off the man's debt out of his own account then hands the man his personal debit card. Everything that was the banker's now belongs to his son, the man once indebted to him. The man leaves the bank not only debt-free but *rich*! He lives the rest of his life in freedom because of his relationship with his new gracious father.

We may acknowledge that we are broken, but accepting our imperfection is only half of the solution. We need the other half of God's promise, the other half of the gospel. Jesus forgives our sins *and then* invites us into his family. Every good thing that belongs to him as the Son of God now belongs to us as well, including his perfection. The Father didn't send the Son so we would live a life of trying to make our spiritual ends meet. Rather, he desires for us to walk in the freedom of a fulfilled and abundant life in Christ.

We no longer must bear the burden to make ourselves perfect on our own. We can, instead, live according to the perfection of Christ in us.

Longing for Perfection

Though we have been covered with the perfection of the ascended Christ, we will continue to grapple with our imperfections until we reach heaven. Every day we will face the sin in our lives and in the world. We will always feel the same tension as Paul did: "Not that I have already reached the goal or am already perfect, but I make every effort to take hold of it because I also have been taken hold of by Christ Jesus" (Phil. 3:12). Even as Christ has perfected us for all time, we still long for the day when we will receive our full inheritance—a sinless body to reign with him in a perfect new creation.[6]

As Christians with this holy longing for perfection, we can put our hope in God's promise to restore his creation to its full goodness. As God the Father declared, "It [is] very good,"[7] over his creation and God the Son cried, "It is finished," on the cross,[8] our triune God will one day proclaim, "It is done!" over his new creation.[9] He will remove the curse of sin and will recreate everything to his perfect design. We will at last be complete and whole in him.

Unfortunately, rather than resting in this perfection of Christ promised to us, we still struggle to do it all on our own.

---

6. Revelation 22:5
7. Genesis 1:31
8. John 19:30
9. Revelation 21:6

We trust in a DIY religion that can never satisfy our longings because we weren't created to perfect ourselves.

Struggling to Do It All

On the final day of 2019, I opened an expensive new goal planner, grabbed a set of colored Sharpie pens, and wrote out how I would make the year 2020 my best yet. After a difficult year of postpartum anxiety, a miscarriage, and a delayed adoption process, I was determined to plan my way into a better year. After hours spent completing the goal-setting prompts with my rainbow of ink, I confidently held my faultless blueprint for 2020 in my hands.

Yet, like for many of you, the following year did not follow any of those "perfect" plans due to a global pandemic. The carefully written goals and intentions were discarded one after another until they littered my mind like dirty face masks in a parking lot. Even though my original goals had fallen by the wayside, I still felt pressure to "make the most" of our time at home during lockdown—bake the bread, keep up the exercise, and build a regular family discipleship routine. I agonized over how I was supposed to do it all, how I could still maintain my goodness during such a difficult and lonely season.

Still, there were a few bright spots over the course of the pandemic—one of which was the sweet FaceTime fellowship with my women's discipleship group. Every Wednesday during my kids' naptime, I propped up my phone on my desk and shared with these women the overwhelming emotional, mental, and spiritual load I carried. While all four of us were in different life stages, they empathized with my struggles, and we collectively carried each other's burdens.

In the darkest days of quarantine, our group began studying the book of Hebrews. Expecting to find a book packed with Old Testament references I wouldn't understand, I instead resonated with the struggle of these first-century Jewish Christians. They, too, wrestled with a "DIY religion" of sorts, feeling tempted to return to the self-righteousness and self-sufficiency of the Jewish law even after they placed their faith in Christ. As I studied, I realized the message that freed these early believers from the legalism of their Jewish culture could also set me free from the heavy burdens of cultural Christianity.

A Shadow of Good Things

The author of the book of Hebrews wrote to a church full of Jewish Christians who were trying to combine the gospel of grace with their religious culture—observing Jewish rituals, offering sacrifices, and accepting the burden of the law. In a similar way, modern Western Christians—inculcated in a culture of independence, industriousness, and individualism—have combined the gospel of grace with our religious performance.

We claim Scripture alone, Christ alone, faith alone, grace alone, and glory to God alone. Yet we also add church attendance, service opportunities, outward obedience, and the curated Instagram image with our Bible and coffee. While those things are *good*, they can never be the source of our goodness. The Jewish Christians believed they needed to continue their religious rites to be accepted, and we have often believed that we need to independently strive to gain God's approval. We must make up for our own inadequacies so we can be whole again.

The author of Hebrews wants us to know that nothing could be further from the truth of the gospel. "Since the law has only a shadow of the good things to come, and not the reality itself of those things, it can never perfect the worshipers by the same sacrifices they continually offer year after year" (Heb. 10:1). No in-depth Bible study, financial sacrifice, or early-morning prayer time can make us perfect. Nothing we do can achieve our own perfection. Any good work that we can do is merely a shadow of the finished work Christ has done on our behalf.

Modern-Day Sacrifices

For much of my Christian journey, I believed I must make modern-day "sacrifices" to gain entrance before a holy God. I must check off my daily Bible reading plan. I must hold my tongue. I must stay pure before marriage and submit to my husband after marriage. I must selflessly serve the church, even to the point of burnout. I must discipline my children's behavior so they would reflect my own goodness.

I continually offered these sacrifices every year, but they could never make me perfect. "Otherwise, wouldn't they have stopped being offered, since the worshipers, purified once and for all, would no longer have any consciousness of sins? But in the sacrifices there is a reminder of sins year after year" (Heb. 10:2–3). Rather than make myself perfect, my self-sufficient efforts only reminded me even more of my own imperfections. Just as the author reminded the church in Hebrews that animal sacrifices could never take away their sin,[10] he reminded me that no quiet time, generous tithe, or mission trip could ever make me right before God.

While studying the book of Hebrews convicted me of my feeble attempts to "do it myself" in my faith, it also opened my eyes afresh to the beauty of the gospel: God never places that burden on his people. My admission into the presence of God is not due to any work I've done, but in the finished work of Christ.

Our perfection was accomplished by the life, death, and resurrection of Christ. We don't have to make ourselves whole because he has already filled us in him.[11] We can lay down our

---

10. Hebrews 10:4
11. Colossians 2:10

useless sacrifices and raise our hands in worship with unburdened arms.

Dressed in Christ's Righteousness

We will always feel the temptation to try and make ourselves right before God. In a culture saturated with messages about creating our own identity, we must fight to hold on to the perfected identity we have in Christ. How do we push back against the demands of our culture to do it all *or* to give up all hope? We look to Christ.

Rather than navel-gazing—feeling pride at our good efforts and shame at our mistakes—we can lift our eyes upward toward the perfection of Christ. We don't have to hope in our own efforts to do it ourselves when Christ has already finished the work to make us whole again.

I have been the woman with completed habit trackers, elaborate meal plans, and inspirational Instagram captions. I have also been the woman in stained leggings, sitting on the couch with a gallon of BlueBell Cookie Two Step ice cream. I have both wallowed in the shame of my imperfections and exhausted myself striving for perfection. Neither woman walked in the freedom of Christ's perfection.

I don't know which kind of person you are today. I don't know if you are afraid that the flawless persona you have constructed will crack under the weight of pressure. I don't know

if you feel ashamed that you can't move past the glaring imperfections you see every morning. Wherever you are today, Christ
extends the hope of his righteousness.

Instead of leaving us in our nakedness or in our crudely fash-
ioned fig attire, Christ has clothed us in white robes, purified by
his own perfect sacrifice.[12] And there is no way we can ever stain
or lose these flawless garments. We rejoice in singing the hymn:

> *When he shall come with trumpet sound*
> *Oh may I then in Him be found*
> *Dressed in his righteousness alone*
> *Faultless to stand before the throne.*[13]

Friend, to fully experience joy in Christ's perfect sacrifice,
we first have to lay aside our own self-sufficient sacrifices.

Growing in Godliness

I can't remember the last time I went to an antique store
and spray-painted a piece of shiplap (three kids will reduce your
time for hobbies), yet I often still feel the need to cover up my
imperfections. When I'm harsh with my kids, I want to pretend the outburst didn't happen rather than humbly apologize
to them. When I forget a commitment to a friend, I want to

---

12. Revelation 7:13–14
13. Edward Mote, "My Hope Is Built on Nothing Less," 1834. Public domain.

make false excuses rather than own up to my mistakes. When I've said something hurtful to my husband, I want to justify my words rather than ask for forgiveness.

Every day I must remember I cannot reach perfection in my own efforts. Rather than do it myself, God invites me to turn to him for my growth in godliness.

"His divine power has given us everything required for life and godliness through the knowledge of him who called us by his own glory and goodness" (2 Pet. 1:3). What empowers our ability to pursue a godly life? Intimate knowledge of the God who has called us. We fight the temptation to live the Christian life in our own strength by growing in our understanding of God and his Word.

As we continue into the next section of this book, we will replace culture's lies of self-righteousness and self-sufficiency with the knowledge of who God is, who we are, and how God is working his salvation in us. We must release the lie that our worth is found in what good we can do and, instead, hold fast to the goodness of Christ.

Remember

When you feel the pressure to do it all and to do it yourself, you can trade your shame and striving for the truth that:

> *I am enough because Christ has made me*
> *completely righteous before God.*

 **Reflect**

1. How do you try to hide your mistakes and failures from others and from God? Why do you think you feel the need to present a "perfect" exterior?

2. What are some modern-day sacrifices in your life? What are good things you feel you must do to win approval from God and others?

3. How can your longing for perfection drive you closer to God instead of farther from him? How can you lay your desire for wholeness in your life at the feet of Jesus?

 Read

For further study, read Philippians 3:3–12. Write down ways that you "put confidence in the flesh" (v. 3)—ways you hope in your own efforts to make you whole. Ask God to help you to "consider everything to be a loss in view of the surpassing value of knowing Christ Jesus" (v. 8). Pray you would rest in the truth that Christ is holding you.

The Truth

PART II

Chapter 3
A Right View of God

I collapsed onto our worn couch—frayed and stained from our small children—and dropped my face into my hands. "Why can't I control my temper?" I groaned aloud. Glancing up at the baby monitor on the coffee table, I watched my children's backs finally rise and fall to the rhythm of sound sleep. My stomach sank, remembering how many times I had failed them that day.

"I am a terrible mother," I whispered to myself.

From the time my eyes first snapped open that morning to the sound of my toddler wailing, I was already running on fumes. My husband was traveling for work, and I struggled to solo parent my two toddlers. The oatmeal boiled over, the kids skipped their naps, the wet laundry sat in the washer, and work deadlines were ignored. Overwhelmed by my imperfection and inadequacy, I lashed out at my children at the smallest inconveniences, scrolled social media to avoid my responsibilities, and sent my husband bitter, snippy texts (even though none of this was his fault).

After the eternally long day, we finally made it to dinner. I stared at the clock on the stove, counting down the minutes until I could tuck my children into bed and put this entire day to rest. I only had to make it through our bedtime routine without sparking a tantrum.

"It's time to clean up," I said nonchalantly, hoping my directive wouldn't trigger my toddler's independent streak.

My daughter's defiant blue eyes met mine. "I don't want to!" she yelled back, causing my son to scream in his highchair.

My tank hit empty, just minutes from the finish line. I threw my own tantrum: "I don't care if you don't want to, you're going to clean up your toys!" I stomped around the house—yelling warnings to my distracted daughter and muttering about my husband not being there. Rather than end the day with a Bible story, hymn, and prayer (as we usually do when my husband is home), our final moments together were filled with salty tears and harsh words.

Finally, my children surrendered to sleep. In the stillness, I felt convicted to pick up my Bible and journal. However, after a day like today, I didn't feel like doing anything, especially my quiet time. I knew I *should* spend time with God, but I didn't *want* to. Besides, after a day like that, I wasn't sure *God* wanted time with *me*.

You're not allowed to make mistakes, Bethany. The crushing words echoed in my heart—words once spoken to me by a church teacher when I was a teenager. *Other people look up to you.* I imagined God shaking his head in disappointment at the way I had treated the precious children he'd entrusted to me. Heat rose to my face and tears pricked my eyes. The burden to be good enough, particularly good enough as a mother, weighed heavy on my shoulders. I sank deeper into the couch cushions. I couldn't bear the shame of coming before my heavenly Father, not when I had been such a horrific mother—and all-around human being—that day.

Maybe reading a book would be better than nothing, I thought. I pulled out a cozy plaid blanket from a wicker basket and steeped a mug of blueberry mint tea. I grabbed a book off the coffee table, *Gentle and Lowly,*[1] and curled up in the corner of my couch. Hiding behind the cover, I hoped God wouldn't find me here, enveloped by my shame.

A Distorted View of God

For the first two decades in my Christian life, I walked on eggshells around God. I checked off my quiet time, served my local church, and followed all the "good Christian" rules—glancing over my shoulder for his approval. I lived as if God were a harsh king, a vindictive judge, and an impatient

---

1. Dane C. Ortlund, *Gentle and Lowly: The Heart of Christ for Sinners and Sufferers* (Wheaton, IL: Crossway, 2020).

parent—demanding my good behavior before offering his affection and kindness toward me. I obviously wouldn't have described him as such, but when I became a mother, my parenting choices began to expose my true views of my heavenly Father.

When I shouted an order from the kitchen and anxiously peeked around to see if my daughter obeyed, I displayed God as a distant king, waiting to see if I follow his commands perfectly. When I quickly spoke a harsh word as my son's toddler brain processed a right or wrong decision, I reflected God as an impatient judge, swift to condemn my incorrect choices. When I placed unrealistic expectations on my children, like swiftly cleaning up their room before bedtime, I showed God to be a demanding father—his love and favor dependent on my good works. My expectations as a mother often revealed my misunderstandings about God as my Father.

When I believed lies about who God was, I also fell for lies about who God expected me to be.

Exposing the Lies

I'm not the first to let a false view of God distort how I live. In the garden, God created man and woman to be in perfect relationship with their Creator, to walk with him and to fully know him. However, they chose to believe falsehoods about

God—that he was holding out on them, that he wasn't who he said he was, and that he didn't know what was best.[2]

Ever since Adam and Eve believed the first lie, humankind continues to make false assumptions about God. While we are made in *his* image, we assume he is like *us*—revengeful and exacting, quick to anger, and slow to forgive. When we run and hide in shame from God, it's often because we do not understand who he truly is.

Tozer wrote: "What comes into our mind when we think about God is the most important thing about us."[3] Maybe you're like me, and you've believed God is disappointed in you when you fail, so you pursue perfection to prove yourself to him. Maybe you believe God only cares about you if you're successful, so you strive harder to gain a glance from him. Maybe you believe God to be cruel or cold like your earthly father, so you avoid interactions with God altogether. Whatever we believe about our Creator will ultimately determine what we believe about his creation—including ourselves.

We must uncover these lies we've believed about who God is. Only then can we trust in who God has revealed himself to be.

---

2. Genesis 3:1–7
3. A. W. Tozer, *The Knowledge of the Holy* (New York: HarperCollins, 1961), 1.

God's Character Changes Everything

Even though I was exhausted from my difficult day, I stayed curled up and reading on the couch long past my bedtime. I turned page after page of the hardbound volume until one page stopped me in my tracks. Rereading it again, my eyes widened, and a rock dropped to the bottom of my stomach.

I snapped the book shut and launched it across the living room—surprising both of my cats who snuggled at my feet. Tears burst from my eyes and my head shook in disbelief. The kind of God the author described seemed outrageous: "Remember that he is the Father of mercies. He is not cautious in his tenderness toward you. He multiplies mercies matched to your every need, and there is nothing he would rather do."[4] How could God love *me* like *that*?

Regaining my composure, I apologized to my cats and picked the book off the floor. I opened to where I had left off and read as the author quoted a passage from Exodus: "The LORD passed before him and proclaimed, 'The LORD, the LORD, a God merciful and gracious, slow to anger, and abounding in steadfast love and faithfulness'" (Exod. 34:6 ESV).

Though I know I had read that Scripture before, Ortlund opened the eyes of my heart to the glorious goodness of God:

---

4. Ortlund, *Gentle and Lowly*, 133.

When God himself sets the terms on what his glory is, he surprises us into wonder. Our deepest instincts expect him to be thundering, gavel swinging, judgment relishing. We expect the bent of God's heart to be retribution to our waywardness. And then Exodus 34 taps us on the shoulder and stops us in our tracks. The bent of God's heart is mercy. His glory is his goodness.[5]

It seemed too good to be true. How could God feel that way about me, especially after how awful I had been that day? I finally finished the chapter, and my heart burst open—ready to accept the unconditional love God was ready to lavish upon me. Though I had been a believer for more than two decades when I read this book, for the first time, I began to know, to love, and to trust God for who he really is.

The Lord Is . . .

"Name one interesting fact about you," the professor stood at the front of the whiteboard, asking us to introduce ourselves on the first day of class. Instantly, my palms began to sweat and my mind raced. I hated when I was asked this question, feeling the pressure to summarize myself in a fascinating nugget. My

---

5. Ortlund, *Gentle and Lowly*, 147.

answer to this question would set the expectations for who I would be during this entire course—and I couldn't think of a single interesting thing about me.

How we introduce ourselves—what we choose to include and/or exclude—reveals something about our character. If I'm truly funny, I will crack a joke in my introduction. If I'm a poet, I will use a beautiful illustration. If I'm a workaholic, I will expound on my accolades. We choose our first impressions and how we present ourselves.

The same is true of God. When Moses asked to see God's glory[6]—to view the fullness of God's character—out of all God's attributes he could have chosen, God revealed himself as "merciful and gracious, slow to anger, and abounding in steadfast love and faithfulness."[7] The prophets echoed God's self-revelation throughout the Old Testament.[8] King David praises God for how he has consistently revealed himself to his people: "The LORD is compassionate and gracious, slow to anger and abounding in faithful love" (Ps. 103:8).[9] These attributes were central to the Jewish view of Yahweh. Is this how we view our God today?

---

6. Exodus 33:18 ESV
7. Exodus 34:6
8. Numbers 14:18; Joel 2:13; Jonah 4:2
9. See also Psalms 86:15; 145:8.

Abounding in Faithful Love

God's holy character is not good news for us unless we believe he is, at his core, love. A God who is omnipotent can move all creation according to his will, but it's only comforting for those who know he loves them and is working all things for their good.[10] A God who is omniscient holds all knowledge, but only a loving God chooses to intimately know his people[11] and share his wisdom with them.[12] A God who is omnipresent may observe all that is done on his earth, but only a loving God chooses to dwell with his people, both in the flesh of his Son[13] and inside them through his Spirit.[14] God's faithful love is central to all his other attributes.

Often, when we read in Scripture, "God is love" (1 John 4:16), we presume he loves like humans do—attaching strings to his affections and goodness. He must love us because we have done good things for him or because we know enough about him. He must love us because we haven't committed certain sins or because we have prayed a certain prayer. However, this is not the kind of love God shows us in Scripture.

---

10. Romans 8:28
11. Psalm 139:1
12. James 1:5
13. John 1:14
14. Romans 8:9

Repeatedly throughout the Old Testament, God describes his love as "faithful." The Hebrew word for his "faithful love," *ḥesed*, can mean goodness, kindness, faithfulness, and steadfastness.[15] It's a covenantal love; God sets his love on his people, not because of their merit, but because of his mercy. His love is based in *his* perfect, faithful nature, not on *our* perfect performance for him. Our "lovableness" is not a prerequisite for his faithful love. Instead, "by loving us, God makes us lovable."[16] We don't have to be enough to earn his love; his love makes us enough. Our worthiness to be loved by him is secure in his perfect character.

We see a picture of God's faithful love in his covenant with Abraham (still called Abram at the time) in Genesis 15. God commanded Abram to cut certain animals in half and lay the pieces opposite one another. In that cultural context, the two members of a covenant or contract would walk between the row of animals cut in half, in essence saying, "Let what happened to these animals be done to me if I don't uphold my end of the contract." In a surprising twist, God put Abram in a deep sleep. God then revealed himself in a smoking fire pot and a flaming torch, and he alone passed between the row of

---

15. James Strong, "ḥesed," *Strong's Hebrew Lexicon (KJV)*, Blue Letter Bible, accessed November 2, 2023, https://www.blueletterbible.org/lexicon/h2617/kjv/wlc/0-1/.
16. James Bryan Smith, *The Good and Beautiful God: Falling in Love with the God Jesus Knows* (Downers Grove, IL: InterVarsity Press, 2009), 105.

slaughtered animals. Because of his faithful love for his people, God promised to uphold both ends of the covenant, even if his people failed.

And they would fail, time and again. Yet God still fulfilled his covenantal promise. God the Son gave his body to be broken on behalf of his sinful people. "God proves his own love for us in that while we were still sinners, Christ died for us" (Rom. 5:8). God does not wait for us to fulfill his expectations before lavishing us with this faithful love. Before we had even taken a step toward him, God's faithful love was running after us.

Slow to Anger

In our culture, God's love is often more palatable—or makes us feel better—than God's anger. This is because we often assume the emotions and actions of God are capricious and selfish like ours.

> When we hear [the word *wrath*] we imagine someone in a fit of rage who has lost all reason and control. . . . So when we speak of the wrath of God, we imagine that God is irrationally full of rage. In the same way that God's love is not a silly, sappy feeling but rather a consistent desire for the good of his people, so also the wrath of

God is not a crazed rage but rather a consistent opposition to sin and evil.[17]

Before we can accept that God is *slow* to anger, we must accept that God can become angry. Just a few chapters before Moses saw the glory of God, three thousand Israelite men were slaughtered for their worship of the golden calf,[18] and God afflicted the remaining Israelites with a plague.[19] Why would God, after performing miracle upon miracle to rescue the Israelites out of Egypt, turn around and judge them? How could we ever draw near to this angry God?

God helps us understand the connection between his wrath and his love in Exodus 34. Whereas he is *abounding* in love, he is *slow* to anger. "His anger requires provocation; his mercy is pent up, ready to gush forth."[20] God's first step to us is always love, and his righteous anger is always an expression of his love.

When we witness the anger of God—whether in Scripture or in life—we can trust his discipline and justice flow from his faithful love for his creation and his people. His love for his people compels him to hate the sin which can destroy them. "God is fiercely and forcefully opposed to the things that destroy his

---

17. Smith, *The Good and Beautiful God*, 120.
18. Exodus 32:27–28
19. Exodus 32:35
20. Ortlund, *Gentle and Lowly*, 148.

precious people. . . . It is a sign of God's love."[21] We see how God's wrath is a sign of God's love most clearly on the cross.

A holy and just God could never let evil go unpunished. Because of his faithful love, he withheld his wrath from sinful people and poured it out upon his own Son. In our shame, we can wrongly believe God the Father is angry at us—the scarred hands of God the Son holding him back. That couldn't be farther from the truth. The Son was sent by the Father. John 3:16 doesn't say, "For God was so mad at the world that he sent his Son."[22] It says, "For God so *loved* the world, that he gave his only Son" (John 3:16 ESV, emphasis added). Jesus is not holding back an angry God. He is the full image of a faithful, loving God who is slow to anger.

We do not have to fear God's anger because Christ has absorbed the wrath due our sin—past, present, and future—in his crucifixion. Instead, we trust God's slow anger is always *for* us even as it is *against* our sin.

Compassionate and Gracious

While God is righteously angry toward sin, he is also compassionate and gracious to his people who sin. God always has sympathy on the frailty of his creation. "As a father has compassion on his children, so the LORD has compassion on those who

---

21. Smith, *The Good and Beautiful God*, 121.
22. Smith, *The Good and Beautiful God*, 99.

fear him" (Ps. 103:13). He knows all our failings, yet he chooses to love us anyway. While we deserve complete separation from God, in his mercy, he makes a way for us to draw near to him.

We don't have to look any further than the life of Christ to understand God's tender heart for his people. His compassion was so great for us, that God the Son chose to leave the glories of heaven and to humbly assume the form of a man.[23] As a human, Jesus could uniquely sympathize with the weakness of our humanity.[24] He could weep and rejoice with us. He could strengthen us and comfort us. Most important, he could make a way for us back to God the Father.

During his earthly ministry, when Jesus stood before a crowd who was hungry for miracles and a word from God, "he felt compassion for them, because they were distressed and dejected, like sheep without a shepherd" (Matt. 9:36). Jesus wasn't frustrated by their misunderstanding. He wasn't disappointed by their sin. He didn't give up on them when they fell away. Rather, Jesus pursued, restored, and redeemed each of his followers.

Jesus sought out the Samaritan woman at the well,[25] called Zacchaeus down from the tree,[26] honored the sinful woman

---

23. Philippians 2:5–8
24. Hebrews 4:15
25. John 4:4–42
26. Luke 19:1–10

who washed his feet,[27] and restored Peter over a fish breakfast.[28] He gave up his very life in the most painful and humiliating way possible so that he might forgive those who crucified him. Jesus's compassion fully displays God's heart of grace toward his people. "Indeed, we have all received grace upon grace from [the Son's] fullness" (John 1:16).

On my worst days, I want to hide from God behind a blanket and book, hoping he'll forget about my failures by the next morning. The beauty of God's grace, though, is that even when we hide—like Adam and Eve did in the garden—he still pursues us. Not to punish with fiery vengeance, but to draw us back to him by his goodness and love. "Only goodness and faithful love will pursue me all the days of my life" (Ps. 23:6).

God's initial response to his people is not judgment or disappointment. It's not anger or impatience. No, his first reaction to our failures is compassion and grace. He doesn't hold us at a distance until we get ourselves together. Instead, he wraps his arms around us to prove he is the one holding us together. His perfect, holy character is able to make us perfect and whole in him.

---

27. Luke 7:36–50
28. John 21:15–19

How Can We Know God?

The more we understand the true nature of God, the more deeply we can draw near to him. When I know his posture toward me is one of love, compassion, and grace, I no longer feel the need to cower in shame when I fail or to strive in my pride trying to earn his approval. God delights in me because *his* love is steadfast, not mine. God desires to be truly known by his people.

Despite humanity's repeated rebellion, God never left his people in the dark about who he was. The book of Hebrews opens with a reminder that God has always revealed himself to his people:. "Long ago God spoke to our ancestors by the prophets at different times and in different ways" (1:1). Throughout the Old Testament, God revealed parts of himself through thunderous storms and gentle whispers; through fire pillars and thick clouds; through judges, prophets, poets, and kings. Still, he veiled his full presence behind a curtain, separating a holy God from his imperfect people. God knew they could not understand the fullest image of who he was through the prophets, so God chose to come to earth himself to reveal his true nature.

When Jesus—the exact imprint of God's glory[29]—came into the world, he changed everything. "In these last days, he

---

29. Hebrews 1:3

has spoken to us by his Son" (Heb. 1:2). God no longer with-held parts of himself from his people. He now displayed him-self fully through God the Son. Through his death, Jesus tore the veil which separated his people from truly knowing him.[30] Now, everything we can know about God is perfectly embodied in Christ.[31]

Because we can know what God is like through Christ, the author of Hebrews wrote: "Therefore, as [Christ] was coming into the world, he said: 'You did not desire sacrifice and offer-ing, but you prepared a body for me. You did not delight in whole burnt offerings and sin offerings'" (10:5–6).[32] God's true desire for his people was never merely sacrifices and offerings. His delight in them wasn't based on their outward practices of religion. No, first and foremost, God has always desired to be known and to know his people.[33] The Jewish sacrificial sys-tem would never be able to accomplish this purpose of God. It may communicate important things about God, but it could never draw his people into intimate relationship with him. His people's minds would always be darkened by sin into believing

---

30. Matthew 27:51

31. Colossians 2:9

32. While the author of Hebrews attributes this quote to Jesus Christ, the Gospels did not record Jesus saying these words during his earthly ministry. However, Jesus was a part of the divine inspiration that led the psalmist to pen these words in Psalm 40:6–8.

33. Hosea 6:6

falsehoods about God's character. They would wrongly suppose God's pleasure in them was based on their performance for him.

Therefore, God the Father sent the Son to rectify this lie with the truth: God himself would fulfill the covenant of his faithful love.

The Love of God Revealed

God knew we could never know him fully on our own. He knew we would never be able to uphold our side of a covenant contract. Before the foundation of the world, God the Father in his compassion, grace, patience, and faithful love planned to send his own Son to offer the final sacrifice for our sin. God's will has never been for his people to earn their way back to God through sacrifices—whether bulls on the altar or quiet times in the morning. His plan of redemption always included the perfect sacrifice of God the Son.

Through his life, death, and resurrection, Christ fulfilled the will of God on our behalf—the will which overflows from his character. "By this will, we have been sanctified through the offering of the body of Jesus Christ once for all time" (Heb. 10:10). The author wanted these Hebrew Christians to know they no longer had to tremble outside a cloud-covered tent. They no longer had to approach God with arms full of bloody animals. They no longer had to meticulously follow rules and rituals.

In the same way, we don't have to tiptoe around God, afraid to arouse his anger. His righteous wrath has been absorbed by Christ's sacrifice. In the loving will of God the Father, we can know him fully through the work of Christ and the power of the Spirit in our lives. Christ's once-for-all offering displayed the perfect character of God. More glorious than the light which shone around Moses on Mount Sinai, Christ's death on the cross proclaimed to all the world, "The LORD is compassionate and gracious, slow to anger and abounding in faithful love" (Ps. 103:8).

God cares for you.[34] He gives you what you don't deserve.[35] He is patient with you when you fail.[36] He delights in lavishing you with his love.[37] He is faithful even when you are faithless.[38] *This* is who God has revealed himself to be to me and to you.

Turn Your Eyes to Jesus

Every day, I wake up to a chorus of vile voices in my head—telling me lies about who God is and what he thinks of me. And every day I have the choice whether to believe these lies or fight back with truth. "Perhaps Satan's greatest victory in your

---

34. 1 Peter 5:7
35. Romans 5:8
36. 2 Peter 3:9
37. 1 John 3:1
38. 2 Timothy 2:13

life today is not the sin in which you regularly indulge but the dark thoughts of God's heart that cause you to go there in the first place and keep you cool toward him in the wake of it."[39] What I choose to believe about God and his love will impact every minute of my day.

When I wake up weary, I can rest in his compassion toward my weakness. When I feel like I can't keep up with the demands of my home, children, and work, I can turn to him for more grace to strengthen me. When I speak harshly toward my children, I can draw near to him in repentance and receive his mercy. When I don't think I can make it to the end of an exhausting day, I can remember his faithful love is holding me. When I feel that knot in my stomach, I get to the root of my shame, fear, or anxiety. I ask myself: *What am I believing about God right now? What does Scripture say about who he is? How does this truth about God relieve me of my shame, fear, and anxiety?*

When we take our eyes off Jesus, the Word made flesh,[40] we are quick to fall for Satan's lies about God's character. We may believe him to be a distant king, an impatient judge, and a demanding father. But when I don't *feel* like I'm enough, I can take my eyes off my myself and lift my eyes to the glorious God who has revealed himself to me. Looking to Jesus, we see God

---

39. Ortlund, *Gentle and Lowly*, 151–52.
40. John 1:14

for who he is: compassionate and gracious, slow to anger, and abounding in faithful love.

If you feel like you're not enough today—if you are drowning in your shame and burdened by striving—ask that God would reveal *his* glory to you. Don't turn your eyes inward, hoping to discover and prove your own worth. Turn your eyes upward to Christ, the one who perfects our faith.[41]

We cannot feel any sort of confidence in who we are until we intimately know the One who made us. As Jen Wilkin often says, "There can be no true knowledge of self apart from the knowledge of God."[42] Only when we have a right view of the God who created us, can we have a right view of who *he* has created us to be.

Remember

When you feel like God is a harsh king, a vindictive judge, and an impatient parent, you can trade your shame and striving for the truth that:

I am enough because God is compassionate and gracious toward me, covering me with his faithful love.

---

41. Hebrews 12:2

42. Jen Wilkin, *Women of the Word: How to Study the Bible with Both Our Hearts and Our Minds* (Wheaton, IL: Crossway, 2014), 26.

Reflect

1. What is the first thing that comes to your mind when you're asked to describe God? How does that perception of God impact how you approach him?

2. Which of the three attributes of God discussed in this chapter is hardest for you to grasp—his steadfast love, his slowness to anger, or his compassionate grace? Why do you think that is?

3. How can you practice turning your eyes to Jesus to see God for who he really is when you are tempted to believe lies about him?

Read

For further study, read Psalm 145. Ask God to reveal any misconceptions about him that remain in your heart. Write down a prayer based on this psalm, praising God for his many wonderful attributes and works. Pray for opportunities to declare his goodness to those around you.

Chapter 4
A Right View of Ourselves

I *love* Monday mornings.

The fresh beginning to a new week. The clean slate in my color-coded planner. The carefully crafted meal plans and ambitious workout goals. The bright-eyed optimism that *this* week, I will finally do it *all* (and, if I'm being honest, do it perfectly). I relish Monday mornings.

Especially this particular Monday morning, the first Monday in *January*. New Year energy tripled my ambitions for a new week. I woke up to my 5:15 a.m. alarm, ready to flawlessly execute my day. I journaled my prayers while my French press coffee steeped. I watched the sun rise as I finished my quiet time. I exercised, showered, and even put on real clothes (not just sweatpants) before I heard my toddlers' bedroom door creak open.

I've got this, I coached myself proudly. And for the most part, the day went according to my plan. We stayed on my newly minted schedule. The kids played happily in the morning while I meal-prepped, and they rested quietly in the afternoon while I worked. I made it through dinner and their bedtime routine without a cross word. I never once sat down, trying to cross out as many to-do items as possible. I had to get it all done today, or I would be behind the rest of the week.

As I lay in bed that night, I felt exhausted physically and mentally, but also accomplished. I felt good. I felt valuable. I felt *fulfilled.* With a deep exhale, I quickly fell asleep. All I had to do to maintain this proud euphoria was to repeat this perfect day tomorrow—and the day after that.

My alarm went off the next day, and my body felt like it had been run over by a truck. I snoozed a half dozen times, finally dragging myself out of bed to take a sip of coffee before my children woke up. Unlike the day before, I couldn't seem to finish a single task. Sick children interrupted my plans. My body refused to keep up with my housework. My mind could barely craft a full sentence. I ended the day with more items on my list than when it had begun.

That Tuesday night, as I lay in my bed, I wracked my brain for what went wrong. I had pushed my body and mind so hard on Monday, I had nothing left to give on Tuesday. (I would later find out I was also sick with a virus.) I chastised myself for not having the stamina to consistently execute a perfect day, seven days a week. I balked at my mental and physical limits—wondering how I could better discipline myself to maintain that pace. How could I live a life of only "motivated Mondays" and not "tired Tuesdays"?

I closed my eyes, worn out and hopeless. I felt like a failure. I felt worthless. I felt like I wasn't good enough.

Who Am I?

When I lay in bed at night, my mind often replays the highlight reels from my day, and I'm tempted to believe these moments are the sum of who I am.

Did my quiet time: +1 point

Yelled at my kids: –1 point

Met a work deadline: +2 points

Left three items undone on my list: –3 points

I do the mental math to discover whether I measured up that day. Maybe you're trained in this mathematic equation as well.

Our view of ourselves can change drastically in only twenty-four hours because we have believed our value is based on our performance each day. "When the day is lovely and sunny and everything is going according to plan, I can look like a pretty good person. But little things gone wrong and interrupted plans reveal who I really am; my cracks show and I see that I am profoundly in need of grace."[1] Rather than accept God's grace, we attempt to hold the cracks together with another to-do list and greater resolve to do it right next time. Ultimately, we believe who we are is what we do.

One of the central questions of any worldview is: *Who am I?* The world answers this question in a myriad of ways. We can be our sexual identity, our career advancements, our clothing size, or our children's milestones. However, when we place our identity in these fleeting places, we will always struggle to feel sufficient and satisfied in who we are. The identities we build on the shifting sands of our own efforts and ability will always fall during life's storms. Thankfully, there is a solid rock on which we can build a firm foundation for our identity.[2]

Who we are can't be self-determined because we were not self-created. We don't have the right to decide who we are because that belongs to the One who created us. "Our identity is rooted in how God made us and in what God speaks over us, not in what we make of ourselves."[3] Our value is not found in whatever external or internal identity statement we make. If we

---

1. Tish Harrison Warren, *Liturgy of the Ordinary: Sacred Practices in Everyday Life* (Downers Grove, IL: InterVarsity Press, 2019), 54.
2. Matthew 7:24–27
3. Jen Wilkin and J. T. English, *You Are a Theologian: An Invitation to Know and Love God Well* (Brentwood, TN: B&H Publishing Group, 2023), 86.

want to finally feel whole, we must understand who God has created us to be.

The world isn't the only one telling false narratives about who we are, though. The church also can often tell us incomplete stories about our identity. As a child in Vacation Bible School, I would often make beaded bracelets as a means of sharing the gospel. Each bracelet had six colored beads symbolizing different aspects of the gospel message. I don't recall what each bead represented, but I do remember the first bead was always black. It signified the truth that we are sinners, and our sin separates us from a holy God. We memorized Romans 3:23—"For all have sinned and fall short of the glory of God"—ready to tell others they were sinners in need of a Savior. The gospel story I wore on my wrist always began with you and me as sinners. Without realizing it, I internalized that the truest thing about me is that I was a sinner. At my core, I was not good.

The doctrine of original sin—that all humanity is born with a fallen, sinful nature—is an important biblical truth, yet it is not where God begins his story of redemption. By starting the gospel with a black bead, telling us we are sinful, we miss critical parts of our human identity. Before the fall of man in Genesis 3, God communicated foundational truths about who we are in Genesis 1–2: we are created good in his image, with good limits, and to do good works.

Created in His Image

Before sin ever entered the story, the eternal triune God spoke the world into existence. He created light and darkness, sky and sea, trees and flowers, sun and moon, birds and fish, animals and insects. On the sixth day of creation, our Creator God did something different. He declared: "Let us make man in our image, according to our likeness. . . . So God created man in his own image; he created him in the image of God; he created them male and female" (Gen. 1:26–27). Instead of speaking man into existence, "the Lord God formed the man out of the dust from the ground and breathed the breath of life into his nostrils, and the man became a living being" (2:7).

God reveals parts of himself in all his creation,[4] but humans more clearly and uniquely reveal truths about their Creator in how he made them. This beautiful truth, called the *imago Dei*, means "we have received [the mission] from God to be his representatives to the rest of creation, to reflect the very character of God."[5]

What distinguishes a woman from the birds in the sky and the flowers in the field is her ability to more clearly display God's love, patience, compassion, and grace. She can be in a relationship with God and others. She can think, speak, and

---

4. Romans 1:20
5. R. C. Sproul, *Everyone's a Theologian: An Introduction to Systematic Theology* (Sanford, FL: Ligonier Ministries, 2014), 103.

build. Jesus himself points to the difference between humans and the rest of creation when he tells the crowds to consider God's care for the birds and the flowers: "Aren't you worth more than they?" (Matt. 6:26). We have inherent value because we are made in God's image.

After God finished his work and prepared for rest, he looked out over all his creation, including humans, and called it, "very good indeed" (Gen. 1:31). Our original design was *very good*. When we ground our identity in the creation narrative, we realize God's work of redemption is not about us trying to earn our way to be good enough. It's about being restored to the full goodness with which God created us.

God's image in each of us is marred by sin, yet we can never lose the image of God in us. Both believers and nonbelievers still reflect God's likeness.

> Image-bearing is not based on usefulness. Image-bearing is not based on ability. Image-bearing is not based on productivity or contribution. Image-bearing means that all humans, regardless of social, intellectual, or physical distinctions, are endowed with divine dignity, value, and worth.[6]

---

6. Wilkin and English, *You Are a Theologian*, 91.

Nothing you can do—or not do—can make you lose this divine dignity, value, and worth. A bad day cannot lessen it any more than a good day can increase it. Our identity as image-bearers is secure because it was endowed to us by our Creator. God made us; therefore, he has the right to declare us good.

Created with Limits

We are made in the image of a limitless God, *and* he created us with limits. God made us embodied, gendered, and dependent human beings. God crafted Adam and Eve into flesh and bone, not just spiritual beings. This means all humanity is limited in time and space by the bodies God has given us. He also made humans distinctly male and female. Our culture may debate over the roles of both sexes, but we will always be limited by what our bodies can and cannot do as women and men. Finally, God designed humanity to need one another. God said, "It is not good for the man to be alone" (Gen. 2:18). Because of his creative design, every human must rely on both God and others—whether they realize it or not—to make it through every day.

As God's image-bearers, we reflect the perfection of God. However, as finite humans, we do so imperfectly. While sometimes our imperfections are consequences of sin, often they are merely a result of our God-given limits. We frequently attempt to push against these limits, wanting to do more than our body, mind, and spirit were created to do—leaving us exhausted and anxious.

"Rather than allowing you to be honest about your finitude, your anxiety tells you that not only should you be able to do everything you imagine needs to be done, but you should do it perfectly. . . . Anxiety confuses limitation with sin, thus convincing us that we are letting God down."[7] We should never be content with the sin in our life, yet often our shame and dissatisfaction about our inadequacy is founded not in a sin issue but in our God-given limitations.

We don't have to experience shame for the ways God has created us. God isn't disappointed when we choose a full night's sleep over finishing another work project. He created our bodies to rest. God isn't frustrated when we must turn down a ministry opportunity because our plate is already full. He knows our minds and hearts can only manage so much. He's not shocked when we need extra care during harder seasons such as chronic illness or the postpartum period. He sympathizes with our weakness.[8]

If we feel like we are not doing enough, we often have unrealistic expectations about what we can do as humans—expectations our Creator never lays on our shoulders. We will always

---

7. Kelly M. Kapic, *You're Only Human: How Your Limits Reflect God's Design and Why That's Good News* (Grand Rapids, MI: Brazos Press, 2022), 132.
8. Hebrews 4:15

find ourselves insufficient when we try to take the place of our limitless Creator rather than humbly serving him as his limited creature.

Created for Good Work

After creating Adam and Eve in his likeness yet with limits, God then gave them purpose: "Be fruitful, multiply, fill the earth, and subdue it. Rule the fish of the sea, the birds of the sky, and every creature that crawls on the earth" (Gen. 1:28). God not only gave us his *image* but also his *work*—to create and to rule over creation.

The cultural mandate to cultivate the earth for God's glory began in Eden, continues now, and will continue into God's eternal new creation. We all were created to participate in God's creative work. Paul sought to teach the Ephesians about their identity in Christ, and he reminded them, "For we are [God's] workmanship, created in Christ Jesus *for good works*, which God prepared ahead of time for us to do" (Eph. 2:10, emphasis added). As Adam and Eve were created to cultivate the earth, Christians are recreated—given new life in Christ Jesus—to cultivate God's kingdom on earth.

"[Work] was part of God's perfect design for human life, because we were made in God's image, and part of his glory

and happiness is that he works."[9] Work is the way we participate in God's glorious mission on earth. However, our work
becomes burdensome when we labor in our own efforts and for
our own glory, instead of abiding in the Spirit to accomplish
God's purposes.

We can't do any good work apart from God's good work
in us. Often, I spin my wheels trying to do a hundred different
things I think I'm *supposed* to do, that I neglect the handful of
areas where God has truly called me to serve. I'm left exhausted
and discouraged, trying to perfectly execute my own plans
rather than God's. Unless I join in the work God is already
doing and has specifically called me to do, I am laboring in
vain.[10] My own strivings will never be enough if I am not walking in the work the Lord has for me.

Our good works should overflow out of our confidence
in our identity as image-bearers and our contentment with
our human limitations. We need not stress when our task list
remains unfinished, feel bitter when the kitchen floors don't
stay clean, or experience shame when our bodies need rest. Nor
do we hopelessly give into laziness and ignore the work God
has given us because we are overwhelmed with the messy house

---

9. Timothy Keller, *Every Good Endeavor: Connecting Your Work to God's Work*
(New York: Viking, 2012), 36.
10. Psalm 127:1–2

or afraid to fail at a project. We can walk in the good work God has set before us because of our secure identity in him.

When We Forget Who We Are

The first two chapters of Genesis may be where our story begins, but unfortunately, our story takes a turn in Genesis 3. Adam and Eve grew dissatisfied with the identity God had given them. They didn't want to just bear God's image; they wanted to be God. They didn't want to rely on him; they wanted to be free of all limits. They chose to live according to what they thought was good, not what God had established as good. And so, from that point forward, our identity as humans has been impacted by our sin nature. We strive to establish our own identities, disregard our boundaries, and work for our own glory. Our identity as image-bearers is secure, however, how well we reflect the image of God is tainted by our sin.

Like Adam and Eve, I often believe Satan's lie that I can be good enough on my own if I only believe in myself, make a plan, and work hard. When I live according to this false narrative, I agree to more ministry commitments, add too many social events to my calendar, and squeeze in another task on an already overloaded day. I ignore the boundaries of my body, mind, and spirit to prove my worth to others and to God. At the end of the day—whether I'm successful or not—I am discouraged and exhausted, because the work is always unfinished. I've faced burnout during several seasons of life because I wanted to be *more* than human; I wanted to be God. "We begin to fall apart physically, emotionally, and spiritually for the simple reason that we are not existing as we were meant to exist."[11]

When I forget who I am—and whose I am—I will never feel like I'm enough.

Never Enough

Just as they needed a reminder about who God is, the audience of the book of Hebrews needed to be reminded about who they were. These early believers were acquainted with deep physical, emotional, and spiritual exhaustion. They had grown up as faithful, observant Jews. They had offered sacrifices, traveled for feast days, and fastidiously kept food and Sabbath laws—all the while facing oppression from the Roman Empire. After believing in the gospel, Christ invited them to set down these heavy burdens and rest in his finished work.

Somewhere along the way, the old habits of self-sufficiency resurfaced. These new believers began feeling the pressure to prove themselves to God and to others by resuming their old rituals and regulations. They wrongly believed their identity could be found in the Jewish laws and ceremonies they followed. Rather than cling to Christ, they were clinging to what

---

11. Hannah Anderson, *Humble Roots: How Humility Grounds and Nourishes Your Soul* (Chicago: Moody Publishers, 2016), 41.

they could do in their own strength. And they were falling woe-fully short.

The author of Hebrews warned them that nothing they could do in their own human efforts would ever be enough. He reminded them of the Jewish priests who were responsible for the draining, daily process of making an entire sinful nation righteous before a holy God: "Every priest stands day after day ministering and offering the same sacrifices time after time, which can never take away sins" (10:11). No sacrifice the priests made would ever be enough to fully take away the stain of sin. How hopeless does that seem—to do a work which will always be unfinished?

I feel this hopelessness in my own daily life, sometimes. There will always be another email to send, dish to wash, and goal to reach. Even more so, my spiritual "to-do" list will always be unfinished in this life. For every sinful desire I seek to root out, three more will pop up in its place. No matter how hard I push, my striving will be as ineffectual as the Jewish priest throwing blood on the altar day after day, year after year. If my identity is in what I can do—for God, for myself, or for oth-ers—I will never be enough.

We Are Dust

In the last chapter, we read in Psalm 103:8 about the glo-rious attributes of God—he is "compassionate and gracious, slow to anger and abounding in faithful love." Additionally, this psalm also gives a word about who we are as humans:

> For [the LORD] knows what we are made of,
> remembering that we are dust.
> As for man, his days are like grass—
> he blooms like a flower of the field;
> when the wind passes over it, it vanishes,
> and its place is no longer known.
> (vv. 14–16)

In contrast to the eternal, immutable nature of our Creator God, we are temporal creatures. Our own feeble and fleeting efforts can *never* make us good enough. *We are dust.*

That's not a Bible verse you typically see printed on a coffee mug or painted on a canvas. It doesn't appear to be encouraging and uplifting to those struggling to find their sufficiency and satisfaction. We would prefer more positive affirmations: *You are beautiful! You are strong! You can do it!* In a self-help culture, to claim such an identity of "dust" seems outrageous and counterproductive.

Friend, this is surprisingly good news for us! The Lord "knows what we are made of," because he made us! He made us in his image and doesn't place the burden on us to create our own identity. He knows our limits and doesn't demand us to surpass them. He doesn't expect our work to last forever, but invites us into his everlasting work.

The sacrifices from the Jewish priests always fell short, and so does our work. We can't declare an identity apart from the one we've been given. We can't muscle our way out of our finitude. We can't make our way outside the sovereign will of God. We're only human, and that's okay, because God created humanity *very good*.[12] We may be dust, but God himself breathed his life into that dust.[13]

You are created. You are limited. You are a part of God's grand plan. Those are better affirmations than this world could ever offer.

Forgetting our identity as God's creation ultimately leads to forgetting our Creator. However, when we turn our eyes back to him, we are then able to see ourselves as he sees us.

The Humility of Christ's Humanity

I could never meet the expectations I had for a perfect Monday, much less a perfect week. I had to learn to accept my humanity. My knowledge and energy will fail and falter. I will run out of hours in the day. I'll never be in two places at once. I'm human—finite, fickle, and fleeting. No internal pep talks

---

12. Genesis 1:31
13. Genesis 2:7

or affirming meditations could change the reality of who I am. And I will never feel content if I am fighting against the way God created me.

Our identity as "dust" does *not* mean we are not valuable. No, the psalmist celebrates the way God knit us together: "I will praise you because I have been remarkably and wondrously made" (Ps. 139:14). Our worth as humans never fluctuates because its reference point isn't found in the dust itself but in the Creator of every dust particle and every hair on our head. His design, limits, and work for me are *good*. He declares me *very good*. He declares *you* very good.

We can find freedom in humble surrender to God's remarkable and wondrous way he made us. "The humility that brings us rest is the same humility that frees us to be the people God created us to be."[14] Humility actually makes us feel *more* sufficient, because our sufficiency is rightly rooted in Christ. Our example for humility can be found in the only perfect human to ever live:

> Adopt the same attitude as that of Christ Jesus,
>> who, existing in the form of God,
>> did not consider equality with God
>> as something to be exploited.
>> Instead he emptied himself

---

14. Anderson, *Humble Roots*, 11.

> by assuming the form of a servant,
> taking on the likeness of humanity.
> And when he had come as a man,
> he humbled himself by becoming obedient
> to the point of death—
> even to death on a cross. (Phil. 2:5–8)

Paul encouraged the Philippians to "adopt the same attitude" toward their own humanity.[15] We don't strive for equality with God—seeking for all knowledge, control, and perfection on our own. Neither do we wallow in shame—disparaging the human weaknesses and limitations Christ willingly took upon himself.

We can take the form of a servant, humbly confident in the identity God has given us. And God promises that as we submit to his will for his creation, he will also raise us up with Christ.[16] He will give us more dignity, honor, and glory than we could ever manufacture in ourselves.

Accepting Our Beautiful Identity

When I accept the way God made me, I can sing with the psalmist, "The boundary lines have fallen for me in pleasant places; indeed, I have a beautiful inheritance" (Ps. 16:6). God

---

15. Philippians 2:5
16. Philippians 2:9–11; Ephesians 2:4–7

has given me specific life circumstances, callings, and capacities. He has set the boundary lines of who I am and who I am not, what I can and cannot do. When I joyfully accept the beautiful way God has created me, I can decline the ministry opportunity outside of my giftings. I can release the world's unrealistic expectations for me to be a "superwoman" doing it all. I can be content with the weakness of my body, the imperfections of my home, and the ordinariness of my calling.

I know who I am on the Mondays where I check every item off the list and on the Tuesdays where I lay sick on the couch. My identity is secure in my Creator, no matter how much or little I do.

> Only when we realize that the world does not depend only on us, . . . only then can we be truly liberated to see that "I am enough." Why? Because I am God's child, and I am connected to his church and world. I have much to offer, but I don't have everything. And God doesn't expect me to, either.[17]

When we walk in the humility of Christ, we can rejoice in the way God made us.

---

17. Kapic, *You're Only Human*, 225.

Living as Beloved Creatures

At the end of the day, our worth is not measured by a completed to-do list, a goal pant size, or a career achievement. These can be good things, but they are not our identity. Our identity as *very good* creations is secure because we are made in the image of God. He has given us good limits and has set good work before us. Nothing we can accomplish *and* nothing we fail to do will ever shake the value our Creator has endowed in us. He loves and accepts us exactly as he created us.

You don't have to prove yourself as a student or employee, wife or mother, or any other identity this world has to offer. You can walk in the remarkable and wonderful identity God has given you as his beloved creature.

You don't have to spin dozens of plates, striving to balance everything. You don't have to do more "good things" to hide your imperfections. You can rest and remember the limits God places around you are good.

You don't have to try to "do it all" to make your mark on this world. No, you can surrender this burden and step into the purpose God is powerfully working in you.

"What will free you from shame is humility; what will free you from shame is accepting that you are not and were never meant to be divine."[18] You are a beloved creature, not the Creator. That is enough.

Longing for More

The reason we often struggle with feelings of inadequacy is because sometimes we are inadequate. We long for perfection because we are imperfect. We are aware of the cracks in our lives and long to be filled. We desire to be perfectly whole like our first parents were in Eden. How can I humbly rest in my identity in Christ while at the same time working to grow in Christlikeness?

To fight the lies of self-reliance and self-righteousness, we don't just need the truth about who God is and who he created us to be that we've learned in these past two chapters. In the next chapter, we will come to understand God's powerful and gracious work inside of us. The God who redeemed us through the death of his Son is also at work in us to transform us into the image of his Son. The God who created humanity by the word of his mouth is also recreating us through the work of his Spirit.

A right view of how God made us will lead us to a clearer view of how he has saved us, is saving us, and will save us once and for all.

---

18. Anderson, *Humble Roots*, 89.

Remember

When you feel frustrated by your human limits and weaknesses, you can trade your shame and striving for the truth that:

I am enough because God created me in his image.

Reflect

1. How would you answer the question, "Who are you?" Do you tend to define yourself by your achievements, your appearance, or your accolades?

2. In the past, have you tended to believe that you were inherently good or bad? How does the fact that you are made in the image of the Creator impact the way you view yourself?

3. Do you feel pressure to be "superhuman"? What would it look like to accept your limitations as a good gift from God?

Read

For further study, read Psalm 139. Write a prayer, praising God for the way that he created you wonderfully and knows you completely. Confess moments where you are tempted to deny the goodness of his creation in your faults and weaknesses. Ask God to remind you in those moments of failure and limitation that he is always with you.

Chapter 5

A Right View of Salvation

I sat among dozens of sweaty, distracted teenagers in a stuffy pastorium-turned-youth house. My youth minister held up a trendy devotional magazine and challenged our group to have a quiet time every day for a month. Anyone who succeeded would receive the prize of a new teen study Bible. I eagerly accepted the magazine he handed out, which included a blank calendar in the centerfold.

Even at a young age, I was already a competitive perfectionist, so I knew crushing the challenge would be no problem. Every morning that month, I slapped my alarm clock and leapt out of bed. I quickly read through the devotional and suggested Bible verses before adding a thick check to the calendar taped to the wall beside my bed.

After thirty days—*perfect* days, I would have said—I walked to the front of the youth room, my thirteen-year-old heart swelling with pride. I handed my youth minister the calendar, precise check marks filling every blank.

"Good job, Bethany!" he praised. "You did it!"

I turned to look out at the room, and the spotlight from the overhead projector blinded me. I squinted to see the approving nod from my Sunday school teacher in the back and the amazed faces of my peers that *someone* had actually read their devotional and Bible every day. My grin reached from ear to ear, and I clutched the new Bible against my chest. I had won the prize.

In my immature faith, the prize wasn't spending time in God's presence, learning more about him, or growing more like Christ. The prize wasn't even the Bible my youth minister had offered as the reward for the challenge. No, the prize for me was the applause from my peers as I stood at the front of the youth room. The prize was my youth minister looking over his glasses and telling me, "Good job, Bethany!" The prize was my inner critic temporarily silenced by my perfect success.

All I wanted at thirteen was to hear my friends, my mentors, the voice inside me, and most of all God say I was good enough.

As always, my pride wore thin, and the praise faded away. I had to keep proving myself over and again. Another devotional book completed. Another mission trip attended. Another student prayer meeting hosted. I thought I would eventually reach a point where I felt secure in who I was. Year after year, my hunger only grew for assurance that I was enough.

If you had asked me then, I would have said I was saved by grace through faith in Christ (and I could quote all the Bible verses to back it up). Deep down, though, I thought I still owed a debt to God. I wanted to show myself worthy of the salvation he had given me.

I knew my eternal salvation was secure. However, I believed the rest of my Christian life here on earth was up to me.

Salvation as a Transaction

That burden to perform perfectly was a heavy load to bear as a teenager, and I still struggle to lay down that burden today. Perhaps it's a burden you carry as well. We fill our Amazon shopping carts with parenting resources, hoping we can successfully disciple our kids. We say "yes" to every opportunity at church, believing we can win the esteem of church leaders. We make lists in goal planners of how we can make ourselves better day after day. These can be good things the Lord has called us to do, but we can be tempted to do them from a place of self-sufficiency and self-righteousness. I still sometimes strive with the same perfectionistic energy which motivated me in my youth, and maybe you do too.

I often feel trapped in "the gap between what Christians claim is true about themselves and what we often see when we look in the mirror."[1] I may acknowledge the truths of God's Word (many of which I've written about in the last two chapters), yet I still oscillate between striving and shame. It's one thing to know the truth, and another thing to live in light of it.

This kind of thinking can relegate the gospel of Christ to a transaction. Christ offers me salvation; I follow his commands. He provides me with new life; I don't waste it. He forgives me of my past sin; I work hard to not sin in the future. Christ gives me a precious gift; I hold onto it until I reach heaven.

This transactional view of salvation is found nowhere in Scripture. The gospel proclaims God's salvation is an unconditional gift we receive by faith in Christ: "For you are saved by grace through faith, and this is not from yourselves; it is God's gift" (Eph. 2:8). Moreover, this saving grace is more than a single moment of conversion. It's the ongoing gift of grace upon grace as the fullness of Christ dwells in us.[2] Christ didn't just give us salvation; he gave us himself. He is our salvation. "Christ did not come to hand us his divine trophy but to carry us in his person across a finish line we could never have crossed on our own."[3]

---

1. Rankin Wilbourne, *Union with Christ: The Way to Know and Enjoy God* (Colorado Springs, CO: David C. Cook, 2016), 33.
2. John 1:16; Colossians 2:10
3. Amy Gannett, *Fix Your Eyes: How Our Study of God Shapes Our Worship of Him* (Brentwood, TN: B&H Publishing Group, 2021), 122.

We aren't alone in our Christian journey because Christ now lives *in us*, and we are *in him*. "I have been crucified with Christ, and I no longer live, but Christ lives in me. The life I now live in the body, I live by faith in the Son of God, who loved me and gave himself for me" (Gal. 2:20). When we view our salvation as more than a one-time gift and as a lifetime spent in union with Christ, we can surrender the burden to make ourselves whole.

Union with Christ

In chapter 1, I shared how Romans 8:1 transformed my relationship with God. When I made mistakes, I didn't have to wallow in self-condemnation because I was "in Christ Jesus." I didn't know it then, but I was beginning to understand how my union with Christ freed me from my shame and striving.

Union with Christ may seem like a vague or mysterious doctrine, but it simply means, "you are in Christ and Christ is in you."[4] Everything that was ours—our sin and shame—now belongs to Christ. And everything that belongs to Christ—his righteousness, his inheritance, his power—is now in us. He takes away our insufficiency and replaces it with his perfect sufficiency.

---

4. Wilbourne, *Union with Christ*, 43.

God "made us alive *with Christ*." "He also raised us up with him and seated us with him in the heavens *in Christ Jesus*." God did this so that "he might display . . . his grace through his kindness to us *in Christ Jesus*." And it doesn't stop there: "we are his workmanship, created *in Christ Jesus* for good works" (Eph. 2:5–7, 10, emphasis added). Every step we take along our Christian journey is firmly rooted in Christ.

You Are in Christ

My oldest daughter loves to cling to her "treasures"—scraps of paper leftover from crafts, a plastic crystal from a tiara, a small stuffed animal that's seen better days. No matter how many beautiful toys I put before her, she often will choose to play with her collection of broken things.

While I laugh at my five-year-old daughter's hoarding, it's not funny when it's me hoarding the broken things within me. My mind keeps a careful catalogue of every mistake I've made. The thoughtless comment I made to a friend which ruined our relationship. The lie I told my boss which he never found out. The bitterly cruel words I spoke to my husband. The (many) times I lose my temper while correcting my children. Even after I've confessed and repented, I often refuse to release these reminders of my inadequacy.

When I cling to these imperfections, I am denying the beautiful gift of my union with Christ. I am in Christ, and he takes all my imperfections on himself—from small mistakes to large offenses, and every sin in my past, present, and future. Christ absorbed it all on the cross. I can lay down my haunting failures at the feet of Jesus Christ and accept the new life he offers me in himself.

"If anyone is *in Christ*, he is a new creation; the old has passed away, and see, the new has come!" (2 Cor. 5:17, emphasis added). Our old self was buried with Christ—along with every mistake we have ever or will ever make—so we could be raised with Christ to walk in this new life.[5] Because we are in him, he confirms our worth. We no longer have to bear the shame for any sin we commit because Christ has given us a new, perfected identity in him.

Christ Is in You

In our union with Christ, he not only takes our shame, he also gives us his glory instead. We have his righteousness[6] and his inheritance.[7] We become fellow heirs with Christ.[8] We gain access to the Father through him.[9] He gives us his power[10] and

---

5. Romans 6:4
6. 1 Corinthians 1:30
7. Ephesians 1:11
8. Romans 8:17
9. Hebrews 10:19–20
10. Philippians 4:13

peace.[11] Everything that Christ has is now ours. We don't need to strive to achieve these. They are a present reality for every believer who is in Christ. We have access to these gifts through the most important gift Christ left us—his very Spirit.

In the final days of Jesus's earthly ministry, he prepared his disciples for when he would leave them: "On that day you will know that I am in my Father, *you are in me, and I am in you*" (John 14:20, emphasis added). How would they know they were united with him? Jesus promised the Father would send the third person of the Trinity, "the Counselor, the Holy Spirit" (v. 26). God the Spirit inside us would be even better than the incarnate God the Son beside us.[12]

The Spirit is the one who applies Christ's work of salvation in our lives: "Now if Christ is in you, the body is dead because of sin, but the Spirit gives life because of righteousness" (Rom. 8:10). For the rest of our lives, we will struggle with the imperfections of our body. We will be weak, we will sin, and we will make mistakes. However, because the Spirit of Christ is in us, we have life through him. God has "put his seal on us and given us the Spirit in our hearts as a down payment" (2 Cor. 1:22). The Holy Spirit guarantees our union with Christ until we at last see him face-to-face in glory.

---

11. Ephesians 2:14
12. John 16:7

When I find myself woefully inadequate in my marriage, my parenting, my work, and my spiritual life, I don't need another pep talk or a positive meditation. No, I need the eyes of my heart enlightened to the hope, inheritance, and power which is already inside of me through my union with Christ.[13] When I'm not enough in myself, I can cling to this gospel hope: "Christ in you, the hope of glory" (Col. 1:27).

Though we have this hope, we will still have days where we fall short of this glory. How can we be confident we are united with Christ when we still make so many mistakes?

Christ's Work of Salvation

A decade after I turned in that perfectly completed calendar to my youth minister, I slowly began to experience freedom through my union with Christ. I realized I couldn't do anything good apart from Christ's work in me. No spiritual service, career accomplishment, or self-improvement could bear any fruit apart from my abiding in Christ.[14] I was no longer trying to earn my salvation on my own. I was living in light of my salvation in Christ.

By centering my salvation around my union with Christ, I could better understand how Christ was at work perfecting

---

13. Ephesians 1:18–19
14. John 15:5

me. "Like the center of a wagon wheel, the doctrine of union with Christ is what supports every other doctrine that encircles it."[15] Theologians typically identify the sequence of salvation to include: "justification, sanctification, and glorification. . . . We were saved, we are being saved, we will be saved."[16]

These may seem like big theological terms that have no bearing on your daily life. In fact, for many years I boasted in my knowledge of these doctrines and was ignorant of the liberation they offered me. However, by digging deeper into these biblical truths, we discover the hope of salvation isn't only for one moment in the past, it's for every day until we reach eternity.

Declared Perfect

On a windy November day, I took my husband's hand, lifted our hefty infant carrier, and walked into the white-stoned county courthouse. Less than an hour later, we walked out with a single slip of paper stating the baby girl in my arms was officially part of our family. She had been loved in our home for six months already, but only the judge had the authority to legally declare this precious child was our daughter through adoption.

Through his sacrificial death, Christ secured the ability to justify us—to declare us perfect in him. Justification means

---

15. Gannett, *Fix Your Eyes*, 122.
16. Jen Wilkin, "How Salvation Brings Freedom," *The Gospel Coalition*, May 10, 2015, https://www.thegospelcoalition.org/article/how-salvation-brings-freedom/.

Christ saved us from the *penalty* of sin once for all.[17] By grace through faith in Christ, we are made righteous before a just and holy God. "Since we have been justified by faith, we have peace with God through our Lord Jesus Christ" (Rom. 5:1). We no longer must suffer the eternal consequences of our sin.

Unlike the Jewish priests who stood day after day offering sacrifices which could never take away sin,[18] Christ "offer[ed] one sacrifice for sins forever [and] sat down at the right hand of God" (Heb. 10:12). In contrast to the priest's *standing* to labor over their *unfinished* work, Christ is now *seated* because he *finished* his work of salvation. We don't have to offer sacrifices of our own good behavior or religious performance to earn God's favor. Christ's one sacrifice for sin on the cross justifies us forever.

Through justification, Christ peels away our filthy rags and clothes us in his pure garments. All our unrighteousness has been credited to him, and he credits us with all his righteousness. When God looks at you, he only sees the shining glory of his Son.

When you feel the weight of your insufficiency, your sin, and your shame, you can stand confidently in the identity Christ has secured for you. Through his single offering, you are perfected in Christ.

---

17. Wilkin, "How Salvation Brings Freedom."
18. Hebrews 10:11

Being Made Perfect

Christ fully paid the penalty for our sin once for all, *and* he is still saving us today. After reminding the readers of their perfection through Christ, the writer of Hebrews points them to Christ's continued work in their lives: "For by a single offering he has perfected for all time *those who are being sanctified*" (Heb. 10:14 ESV, emphasis added). Sanctification means Christ is currently saving us from the *power* of sin over our life.[19] We are no longer slaves to our sinful desires. The Spirit of Christ in us empowers us to walk in his righteousness a little more day by day.

Scripture repeatedly reminds us of this partnership between the work of the Spirit and our own efforts: "Work out your own salvation with fear and trembling. For it is God who is working in you both to will and to work according to his good purpose" (Phil. 2:12–13). We work because God is at work in us. "I labor for this, striving with his strength that works powerfully in me" (Col. 1:29). We strive with God's strength in us.

Christ didn't step in to save us then leave the rest of our Christian life up to us. Every step of our spiritual growth is a gift from him. "We do not find some gifts, like justification, in Christ and then other gifts, like sanctification, in ourselves or even in the Spirit apart from Christ. . . . They are

---

19. Wilkin, "How Salvation Brings Freedom."

given together—with every other blessing—through faith in Christ."[20]

How can we tell the difference between our self-sufficient striving and Spirit-empowered sanctification? "[The] difference between self-help and sanctification . . . is the motive of the heart."[21] When I say yes to a ministry opportunity, try a new method of discipling my children, or practice self-discipline to root out sin in my life, I must examine my motives. Am I doing this to make myself perfect? Or because I have already been made perfect in Christ? The first motivation leads to shame and striving. The latter leads to life and peace.[22]

When you are frustrated by the slowness of your sanctification and by your lingering imperfections, you can remember that Christ is always actively at work in you, making you perfect like him.

Will Be Perfect

I'm only in my mid-thirties, and I can already feel my body fading. My brain needs a full night of sleep to properly function, my stomach can't handle fried foods, and my neck is sore after an hour staring down at my laptop. I take copious

---

20. Michael Horton, *Pilgrim Theology: Core Doctrines for Christian Disciples* (Grand Rapids, MI: Zondervan, 2011), 304.
21. Jen Wilkin, *In His Image: 10 Ways God Calls Us to Reflect His Character* (Wheaton, IL: Crossway, 2018), 148.
22. Romans 8:6

amounts of vitamins, layer serums and moisturizers on my face, and lift light weights to maintain my mobility. Despite all this, I know—unless the Lord comes back before then—my body will continue to weaken until it dies. That is the curse of sin on this earth, but as Christians, we can look forward to a greater hope to come.

Christ has saved us from the penalty of sin once for all, and he is continuing to save us from the power of sin over our lives. One day, through glorification, Christ will ultimately save us from the *presence* of sin forever.[23] "Death will be no more; grief, crying, and pain will be no more, because the previous things have passed away" (Rev. 21:4). Christ will fully and finally remove the curse of sin, and we will be perfectly united with him forever.

In heaven, our desire for perfection will be fulfilled in Christ. We will at last become completely whole as we behold our perfect God: "Dear friends, we are God's children now, and what we will be has not yet been revealed. We know that when he appears, we will be like him because we will see him as he is" (1 John 3:2). We will always battle against our sin on earth. When we dwell with God's presence in heaven, our sinful nature will finally be removed from us. Every niggling doubt,

---

23. Wilkin, "How Salvation Brings Freedom."

lingering temptation, and imperfect crack will be removed. We will stand before our holy God, whole in him.

When you feel the longing for perfection—when you wish you could be free of the intrusive thoughts, bitter words, and inadequate actions—turn your eyes to glory. Look to Christ seated on his throne. Let your longing for perfection kindle a greater desire for heaven. Rejoice that one day in Christ you will receive the goal of your faith: the final, perfect salvation of your soul.[24]

As we trust Christ's work in us through justification, sanctification, and glorification, we can surrender our own striving to make ourselves perfect. Through our union with Christ, we can be confident that the power which saved us is the same power transforming us and sustaining us until the end.

The Spirit's Testimony

My imperfections still come back to haunt me. I get a poor review at work. My efforts at potty training my toddler fail. I can't bring myself to open my Bible. When I struggle to feel like I'm enough, the Holy Spirit testifies about the perfect work of Christ in me.[25] As Christ promised, the Spirit "will teach you all things and remind you of everything I have told you"

24. 1 Peter 1:8–9
25. Hebrews 10:14–15

(John 14:26). I can tune out the enemy's lies telling me I'm not doing enough to prove myself and, instead, listen to the voice of the Spirit reminding me of God's promise:

> "This is the covenant I will make with them
> after those days,
> the Lord says,
> I will put my laws on their hearts
> and write them on their minds." (Heb. 10:16)

This new covenant was God's plan of salvation all along. He gave Adam and Eve one rule, and they disobeyed. He made a promise to Abraham, and Abraham tried to accomplish it on his own. God delivered the Israelites out of Egypt, and they crafted the golden calf. He secured Israel a land, and they turned to foreign gods. God gave Israel a king, and the king rebelled against him. God gave them the law, the sacrificial system, and the feasts, and they still forgot him. God's people could never fulfill God's plan of salvation on their own.

Friend, God knew from the beginning that we never could redeem ourselves. God knew we could never earn salvation on our own. We could never make ourselves perfect. We didn't need a more detailed list of rules. We didn't need stern discipline. We needed new hearts. We needed renewed minds. We needed his Spirit inside of us.

Our union with Christ through the gift of his Spirit is the fulfillment of Jeremiah's prophecy, which the writer of Hebrews quotes:

> "This is the covenant I will make with the house of Israel after those days"—the LORD's declaration. "I will put my teaching within them and write it on their hearts. I will be their God, and they will be my people. No longer will one teach his neighbor or his brother, saying, 'Know the LORD,' for they will all know me, from the least to the greatest of them"— this is the LORD's declaration. (Jer. 31:33–34)

No longer do we experience God's presence *outside* ourselves—operating through clouds and fire, through words carved in stone, and through an ark behind a curtain. God's very presence came to dwell *inside* us, and he writes his laws on our hearts. Now, God guides us, teaches us, and communes with us through his Spirit in us. We can fully know him and be known by him through our union with Christ.

No More Offerings

Christ has declared you and me perfect, is making us perfect, until we reach full perfection in heaven. Therefore, God promises, "I will never again remember their sins and their lawless acts" (Heb. 10:17). If God doesn't remember your mistakes, why should you? You don't have to let your stomach churn over a failure at work, or your mind replay the moments when you yelled at your kids. You don't have to hold onto the sins of your past after you repent, because God has removed them "as far as the east is from the west."[26]

God does not hold a single infraction against you. There is nothing left for you to do to accomplish your salvation. "Now where there is forgiveness of these [sins and lawless acts], there is no longer an offering for sin" (Heb. 10:18). God is not waiting at the front of the classroom for you to turn in your perfectly checked assignment. He's not expecting you to prove your worth by being the best spouse, parent, student, or employee. He's not waiting anxiously at the finish line, wondering if you'll stumble through to the end. No, your perfection is secure in Christ. You are secure in Christ.

This isn't an excuse to kick back and do whatever you want for the rest of your Christian life. The apostle Paul warned about presuming upon the grace of God.[27] Rather, you and I can walk in the new life Christ has accomplished for us. "For if we have been united with him in the likeness of his death, we will certainly also be in the likeness of his resurrection" (Rom. 6:5). We find new life—new hope, new joy, and even new good

---

26. Psalm 103:12
27. Romans 6:1–4

works—through our union with Christ. We can walk in obedience to Christ without the pressure to make ourselves whole.

Christ Holds Us Fast

I wish I could go back two decades and sit down on my purple and lime-green bedspread next to my teenage self. I'd wrap my arms around her and tell her there is a greater prize than anything she could chase in this world. She doesn't have to prove she is worthy of the salvation freely given to her. She doesn't have to earn God's love and approval. She no longer must bear the shame of her mistakes. Instead, she can walk in the perfection Christ has given her.

I can't change the past, but I can remind myself today of the work Christ has done and is doing on my behalf. When I'm tempted to run after a perfect body, perfect children, perfect spiritual disciplines, or a perfectly written article, I must remember the greater prize ahead of me.

> Not that I have already reached the goal or am already perfect, but I make every effort to take hold of it because I also have been taken hold of by Christ Jesus. Brothers and sisters, I do not consider myself to have taken hold of it. But one thing I do: Forgetting what is behind and reaching forward to what is ahead, I pursue as

my goal the prize promised by God's heavenly
call in Christ Jesus. (Phil. 3:12–14)

We can let go of our past mistakes and press on to the
promise we have in Christ. On our own, we could never "take
hold" of the prize set before us—perfect union with God. Our
only hope is in Christ who will hold us fast until he calls us
home.

Friend, if you are weary from holding it all together today,
you can let go because Christ is holding you fast through your
union with him. You don't have to prove you're enough to him,
to others, or to yourself, because he has already declared you
perfect and is making you perfect day by day. And one day, you
will stand before him perfectly satisfied and sufficient in him.[28]

Great and Precious Promises

Because you are united with Christ, his Spirit dwells in
you and helps you to "be transformed by the renewing of your
mind" (Rom. 12:2). In this second section, we have learned how,
by the power of the Spirit, we can fight the enemy's lies with
the truth about who God is, who you are, and how God is saving you and can replace them with gospel truths.

When you fear God is disappointed with your failings,
remember our God is compassionate and gracious, slow to

---

28. 2 Corinthians 3:18

anger, and abounding in faithful love.[29] When you are frustrated with limitations, remember you are made in God's image, with good limits and for good works.[30] When you struggle to live the perfect Christian life on your own, remember Christ has given you his perfection even as he is transforming you to be more like him every day.[31]

As we move into the third and final section, let us consider the "very great and precious promises" (2 Pet. 1:4) that come from believing these truths: assurance of faith, enduring hope, love-motivated good works, and biblical community. We can leave behind the fleeting assurances and applause of this world and press on toward these ultimate prizes we have in Christ.

Remember

When you feel you must prove your worthiness to be saved, you can trade your shame and striving for the truth that:

*I am enough because Christ
has perfected me for all time.*

---

29. Exodus 34:6
30. Genesis 1:26–28
31. 2 Corinthians 3:18

Reflect

1. Do you struggle with viewing your salvation as a "transaction" with God? How have you felt like you "owed" God for the grace he's shown you?

2. What mistakes and regrets can you release because you are in Christ? What gifts can you joyfully receive because Christ is in you?

3. How does the fact that Christ has "perfected you for all time" change the way you pursue growth in your life?

Read

For further study, read Ephesians 1:3–14. Praise God for the way he works in you at every stage of salvation. He chose you, forgave you, and sealed you! Confess moments when you try to earn your salvation by your own works. Ask God to help you know when you are obeying him out of self-sufficient striving or Spirit-empowered sanctification.

The
Promise

PART III

Chapter 6
Assurance of Faith

"Are you happy with me?" I barely whispered the question. My eyes looked down at my hands, and I picked at the dried cuticles on my thumb.

My husband sat next to me on the couch, engrossed in reading a book on his phone. He grunted in reply, "Huh?"

I cleared my throat and asked again, louder this time, "Are you happy with me?"

My husband looked up from his phone, face bewildered. "Um, yeah," he answered slowly, clicking off his phone screen. "Why wouldn't I be?"

I closed my eyes, and clips of the evening's festivities replayed in my head. We had attended a church event for the first time since the pandemic had kept us at home. I had thought the evening would be fun and freeing, but it ended up with our uncontainable fifteen-month-old son scattering papers and pens across the floor, and our three-year-old daughter breaking down in tears because she couldn't have another cookie.

"I forgot to put the water and snacks in the kids' bag, so they got hangry," I began. "And I can't believe I made that awkward comment to our friends. And I know you didn't want to leave early, but I was just so tired."

"Those things weren't your fault. You don't need to apologize," he said, pulling me close. Then he added, "And even if they were, the kids still had a great time tonight. *I* had a great time tonight."

"But it's not just tonight," once I started, the self-accusations continued pouring out of my heart and my mouth: *I can't keep the house clean, can't stay on top of my work deadlines, can't get back into my prepregnancy shape, can't stay consistent with my morning quiet times, can't control my temper. I can't keep it all together.*

I finally came up for air to take a deep breath and to ask the question that had been lurking in the corners of my mind: "How can you be happy with me when I'm messing up so much?"

"Dear, we all make mistakes. It was just a rough night," my husband rubbed my back reassuringly. "I don't blame you at all for any of those things."

Tears threatened my eyes as I tried to believe his gracious words. "But I blame myself. I just don't feel like I'm a good wife or mom or Christian or anything right now."

"How many times do I have to tell you I think you're the *best* wife, mom, and everything?" he teased, kissing the top of my head.

I replied in all seriousness, "Every day, multiple times a day."

He chuckled and held me even tighter in his arms. I knew my husband—a man of few words—was trying to communicate how much he loved me and how he saw me. He was trying to reassure me that I was safe with him, cherished by him, and accepted by him—faults and all.

I never doubt that my husband loves me. He is one of the most steadfast and faithful people I know. However, as the uncertainties and fears creep into my mind, I often need reassurance that he's happy with me. That he doesn't begrudge the woman he's covenantly committed to for the rest of his life.

His kind words and gentle embrace temporarily soothed the nagging doubt in my mind. Yet I wanted more assurance, more proof that I am enough in his eyes.

Even more, I want to know I'm enough in Jesus's eyes. While I have no doubt that Jesus loves me, I'm not always sure that he likes me.

Once Saved, Always Saved

Maybe you have wrestled with these same doubts. When it comes to the assurance of our faith, we often cling to the simply stated doctrine of the perseverance of the saints: "once saved, always saved." Growing up in a faithful Southern Baptist church, this truth was drilled into my mind as a young girl. I held onto the comforting words of my Good Shepherd, "I give them eternal life, and they will never perish. No one will snatch them out of my hand" (John 10:28). Yet we struggle to grasp the implications of this doctrine.

I believed, at least in my head, the truth of salvation which I wrote about in the last chapter. "The full doctrine of 'eternal security' is that once we are saved, we will always be saved, *and* that those who are saved will persevere in their faith to the end."[1] I knew no matter what I did or didn't do, I could never lose my salvation.

I found, however, that I could lose the assurance that came *from* my faith.

Merriam-Webster defines *assurance* as "confidence of mind or manner: easy freedom from self-doubt or uncertainty."[2] I was confident that I had been saved for all time (though I have even struggled with doubts about that at moments in my life). Yet I lacked confidence in how I could approach God as someone he had saved. I didn't have a boldness to approach God freely without self-doubt or uncertainty.

---

1. J. D. Greear, *Stop Asking Jesus into Your Heart: How to Know for Sure You Are Saved* (Nashville: B&H Publishing Group, 2013), 86.
2. *Merriam-Webster*, s.v. "assurance," https://www.merriam-webster.com/dictionary/assurance.

Because I didn't have this assurance of faith, I tended to either pridefully saunter into his presence, boasting in my own merit, *or* cower in the corner, overwhelmed by the weight of my own insufficiency. Neither of these ways is how God designed for his people to come before him.

True Confidence before God

As Christians, we don't have to approach God in self-sufficient striving or in self-condemning shame. In his letter to the church in Philippi, the apostle Paul exhorted believers to "not put confidence in the flesh" (Phil. 3:3). Paul could have boasted in an array of spiritual accomplishments. He was "circumcised [on] the eighth day; of the nation of Israel, of the tribe of Benjamin, a Hebrew born of Hebrews; regarding the law, a Pharisee" (v. 5). Yet he "considered [these gains] to be a loss because of Christ" (v. 7). He knew his ultimate righteousness—his confidence before God—did not come from his obedience to rules but through his faith in Christ. When Paul drew near to God, he did not boast of his own work but of the work of Christ in him.[3]

In his letter to Timothy, Paul provided a different personal résumé: "I was formerly a blasphemer, a persecutor, and an arrogant man" (1 Tim. 1:13). Just as Paul didn't boast in

---

3. 1 Corinthians 1:31

his accomplishments, neither did he let his sins and struggles keep him from the presence of God. Even though he had been the worst of sinners,[4] Paul could stand confidently before God because "the grace of our Lord overflowed, along with the faith and love that are in Christ Jesus" (v. 14). Neither his past achievements nor his failures drew him near nor kept him from full assurance of his faith. Both in his strengths and in his weaknesses, he clung to the goodness of Christ for his boldness before God. "Such is the confidence we have through Christ before God" (2 Cor. 3:4).

We often lack this kind of spiritual confidence. We have been assured that God saved us, but we still doubt that he desires to be close to us. We're tempted to look at our efforts and wonder if they are enough to draw us near to God or to push us away from God. How can we, like Paul, approach God with such confidence? How do we draw near to God with "full assurance of faith" (Heb. 10:22)?

How Can We Approach God?

One way to trace the overarching story of Scripture is to see how God's people have communed with God's presence in God's place. In the beginning, God created a garden where man and woman had unmitigated, unlimited, and unashamed access

---

4. 1 Timothy 1:15

to their Creator. Once sin entered the world, though, God's people could no longer draw near to him as they had in the garden. They would need a mediator, someone who had been cleansed from his sin and could represent a sinful people.

One such mediator was Moses. After delivering the Israelites out of Egypt, God met with Moses on Mount Sinai to give him guidelines for how to prepare God's people for God's new place, the Promised Land. Moses instructed the Israelites to consecrate themselves—to make themselves clean and set apart for God's presence. Even with these rituals, they could only get so close to God on the mountaintop. God told Moses, "Put boundaries for the people all around the mountain and say: Be careful that you don't go up on the mountain or touch its base. Anyone who touches the mountain must be put to death" (Exod. 19:12). To enter fully into the presence of God would mean death.

It's no wonder, then, that the Israelites responded with a healthy fear of the Lord. "All the people witnessed the thunder and lightning, the sound of the ram's horn, and the mountain surrounded by smoke. When the people saw it they trembled and stood at a distance" (20:18). While Moses climbed the mountaintop to behold the glorious presence of God, the Israelites' sin and uncleanness kept them at a distance.

Later, God provided instructions for how he would dwell with his people in the Promised Land.[5] His presence would rest in a cube-shaped room, the Most Holy Place, at the center of the tabernacle or temple surrounded by heavy curtains. One male Levite, the high priest, would be the new mediator between God and his people. Only he would be able to enter this inner sanctuary and only once a year.

The high priest would go through rounds of ritual cleansing and offerings to spend mere moments in the presence of God. The priest would approach the ark of the covenant, where God's presence dwelt, and would sprinkle blood on the mercy seat to cleanse the people from their sin. While he reverently entered through the veil into the presence of God, the rest of the Israelites would gather in the surrounding courts, praying these sacrifices would atone for their sin and make them right before God.[6]

This sacrificial system was not enough to keep the nation of Israel faithful to their God, though. Therefore, God sent judges, kings, and prophets to call the people to repent and to draw the people back to himself. One prophet, Isaiah, "saw the Lord seated on a high and lofty throne, and the hem of his robe filled the temple" (Isa. 6:1). Seraphim flew around the throne, singing of God's holiness, power, and glory.

---

5. See Exodus 25–27.
6. See Leviticus 16.

Isaiah trembled in the presence of God and cried, "Woe is me for I am ruined because I am a man of unclean lips and live among a people of unclean lips, and because my eyes have seen the King, the LORD of Armies" (v. 5). One of the seraphim descended on him and touched Isaiah's mouth with a glowing coal from the altar to purify him. "Now that this has touched your lips, your iniquity is removed and your sin is atoned for" (v. 7). After this purification, God called Isaiah to preach the good news that God would one day again dwell with his people.

If the story had continued as it were, God's people would need one mediator after another to go into the presence of God on their behalf. They would never have confidence to approach God on their own.

I know how the Israelites felt at the outskirts of God's presence. I've been at the base of the mountain, afraid to come before a holy and just God. I've been on the outside, praying that a church leader would tell me that God was pleased with me. I've been face down in God's presence, ashamed of my own impurity. I knew there was no way I could make myself good enough to draw near to him.

Since the beginning, God was at work to bring a better priest, prophet, and king. A mediator that would go before us to the throne of God and would give us the assurance that we, too, could draw near to God's presence without fear or shame.

One who could make a new way for us through the curtain that separated God from his people.

A New Way through the Curtain

One winter afternoon, my children curled up next to me on the couch as I cracked open the cover to a new children's picture book, *The Garden, the Curtain, and the Cross.* As I began reading, I thought to myself, *How funny to have a children's book about the Jewish temple.* As I continued reading, though, my heart was gripped by the temple's impact on the gospel story, especially the curtain surrounding the Most Holy Place.

My children *oohed* and *aahed* over the colorful illustrations, and my eyes pricked with tears at the truth of what I was reading. "For hundreds of years, the temple curtain reminded people that God said, *It is wonderful to live with him, but because of your sin, you can't come in.*" There was a KEEP OUT sign that kept God's people from coming into his presence. We could never make ourselves good enough to enter his presence.[7]

However, God already knew we could never, in our current sinful state, dwell with him. So he came to dwell with us.[8] When Jesus was born into the world, fully God and fully man,

---

7. Carl Laferton, *The Garden, the Curtain, and the Cross: The True Story of Why Jesus Died and Rose Again* (Epsom, United Kingdom: The Good Book Company Ltd., 2016), 15.
8. John 1:14

he fulfilled the role of our final mediator. He lived a sinless life and died to pay for our sins. In Jesus's final moments on the cross, he cried out, "It is finished"[9]—the perfect sacrifice had been made once and for all.

"Suddenly, the curtain of the sanctuary was torn in two from top to bottom" (Matt. 27:51). The thick, indestructible veil of the Most Holy Place, which had separated God's people from God's presence for millennia, was split wide. "God had ripped up the KEEP OUT sign! God's wonderful place is open again! Because Jesus died, we can go in!"[10]

Now we don't have to cower at the base of a mountain, at the edge of a camp, or face down in the dirt. Instead, "we have boldness to enter the sanctuary through the blood of Jesus" (Heb. 10:19). Through his death, Jesus "inaugurated for us a new and living way through the curtain (that is, through his flesh)" (v. 20). Even in our awe and reverence of God's holiness, we can enter the presence of God boldly, freed from any self-doubt or uncertainty.

Boldness to Draw Near

There are days I still come trembling before the presence of God. I pull out my Bible at night and feel nagging shame that

---

9. John 19:30
10. Laferton, *The Garden, the Curtain, and the Cross*, 24.

I haven't been as diligent in my quiet times. I fall before him exhausted from striving to fulfill his callings in my own effort. I beg for forgiveness for all the ways I've failed my family. I approach God like those conversations I often have with my husband, pleading with him, "Are you happy with me?"

The audience of the book of Hebrews struggled with this same doubt too.

In the previous section of this book, we read how the author of Hebrews wrote about three profound truths: who God is, who we are, and how he is saving us. Now, the author wants his readers to live in light of these truths by encouraging them with three "let us" statements. In the next four chapters, we'll explore how we can walk in these promises of Christ.

"Since we have a great high priest over the house of God, *let us* draw near with a true heart in full assurance of faith, with our hearts sprinkled clean from an evil conscience and our bodies washed in pure water" (Heb. 10:21–22, emphasis added). Because of Christ, God doesn't see me as a dirty and imperfect sinner groveling before him with mediocre accomplishments. No, he sees me as his clean and pure daughter. My perfect High Priest, Jesus Christ, has removed the burden of shame from my imperfections, and now I can come before God assured in my perfection in him. I don't have to keep bringing up my past sins and mistakes, because God chooses not to hold them against me anymore.[11] Christ's sacrifice has cleaned my heart and washed my body—he has transformed me from the inside out.

Our inevitable failures need not shake our confidence, because we have assurance to approach the throne of grace through the work of our perfect High Priest. "We can bring our up-and-down moral performance into subjection to the settled fixedness of what Jesus feels about us."[12] Our value as beloved children is firmly fixed in the perfection of Christ.

Friend, we can draw near with boldness because God *always* accepts you and me. Because we are clothed with the perfection of Christ, God looks upon us and is always pleased with us. While we may disappoint our family, our coworkers, or even ourselves, we can never lose the acceptance of our heavenly Father. Even when we sin and he disciplines us as his beloved children,[13] God *still* delights in us. We can never mess up so badly that God will give up on us.

Because of this we can draw near to God, confident that he will always draw near to us.[14] Our assurance of faith means we no longer must seek for assurance in our grades, our work, our parenting, our image, or anything else we can accomplish. When the laundry baskets overflow, we have boldness to draw

---

11. Hebrews 10:17
12. Dane C. Ortlund, *Gentle and Lowly: The Heart of Christ for Sinners and Sufferers* (Wheaton, IL: Crossway, 2020), 187.
13. Hebrews 12:6
14. James 4:8

near to God. When we receive a negative review at work, we have boldness to draw near to God. When our children stray from the faith, we have boldness to draw near to God. When our bodies are frail and fail, we have boldness to draw near to God.

When we feel like we aren't enough, we can walk confidently in the promise that Christ has made a way for us to draw near to God.

Face-to-Face

After teaching the church at Corinth about the sufficiency of Christ, Paul reminds them, "Since, then, we have such a hope, we act with great boldness" (2 Cor. 3:12). Assured in our faith, we don't let anything keep us from the presence of our God. Our sin and suffering, our pride and shame, and our doubts and fears can no longer separate us from the presence of God. And there is still a greater hope to come. Here on earth, we only see a dim reflection of God's glory, but one day, we will see him fully face-to-face.[15]

In the final throne room scene in Scripture, the apostle John sees a new heaven and earth—a new place for God's people.[16] There, we will have unmitigated, unlimited, and unashamed

---

15. 1 Corinthians 13:12
16. Revelation 21:1–8

access to our Creator. "Look, God's dwelling is with humanity, and he will live with them. They will be his peoples, and God himself will be with them and will be their God" (Rev. 21:3). We won't come before God in fear, though, but in worship. We will forever "draw near with a true heart in full assurance of faith" (Heb. 10:22) through the blood of the perfect sacrifice, the Lamb of God.

The doctrine of the perseverance of the saints is so much more than the phrase, "once saved, always saved." The ultimate hope of our perseverance is the promise of entering God's full presence once and for all. This is *how* we persevere.

> Perseverance is not the result of *our* determination, it is the result of God's faithfulness. We survive in the way of faith not because we have extraordinary stamina but because God is righteous, because God sticks with us. Christian discipleship is a process of paying more and more attention to God's righteousness and less and less attention to our own.[17]

We can become more assured in our faith when we pay more attention to the perfection of Christ than our strivings for perfection or our shame from imperfections. We can draw

---

17. Eugene H. Peterson, *A Long Obedience in the Same Direction: Discipleship in an Instant Society,* 2nd ed. (Downers Grove, IL: InterVarsity Press, 2000), 132.

near to God as his beloved children because he is our loving heavenly Father.

Our Abba Father

I once heard author and mother Abbey Wedgeworth encourage parents to always smile at their children first thing in the morning.[18] Even if children wake up an hour early, interrupting your time with the Lord. Even if they start your days with cries for breakfast. Even if they awake almost as grumpy as you feel. By smiling at your children—no matter the less-than-ideal circumstances—we as parents communicate that our primary, most foundational posture toward our children is delight.

Early in the morning, I hear the patter of feet down our hallway and see tuffs of blonde hair creeping around my bedroom doorway. I open my arms and lift my lips into a smile. I welcome my children into my presence because they are *mine*. I love them. They don't have to wait until the perfect time or circumstances to come into my room. While I may follow my embrace with an instruction to go back to their room or to wait for breakfast, I never want my kids to fear coming into my presence. I want them to be assured in their relationship to me.

If I, an imperfect parent, love my children this way, how much more does our heavenly Father love us in this way.[19] "God

18. Abbey Wedgeworth, Instagram.com/abbeywedgeworth.
19. See Luke 11:11–13.

wants us to have certainty about our salvation. He changes, encourages, and motivates us not by the uncertainty of fear, but by the security of love."[20]

Christ's sacrifice didn't just remove the penalty and power of sin in our lives, it restored us to fellowship with our Father. It took our fear and replaced it with the boldness of a child. "For you did not receive a spirit of slavery to fall back into fear. Instead, you received the Spirit of adoption, by whom we cry out, "*Abba*, Father!" (Rom. 8:15).

We don't fear him as a hard master. We run to him as our loving Father.

Friend, when you fear that you are not enough to enter the presence of God, cry out to your good Father. I know that in our broken world, many of you may not have had healthy representations of what fatherly love looks like. Rather than assurance of his love, your earthly father may have instilled fear and shame into your heart as a child. Your earthly father may have been abusive or detached, domineering or absent. That's not the kind of relationship the heavenly Father wants with you.

Our God is love, and he demonstrated his love by sending "his one and only Son into the world so that we might live through him" (1 John 4:9). When we could not on our own draw near to him, he drew near to us. He adopted us, chose us,

20. Greear, *Stop Asking Jesus into Your Heart*, 13.

before we could ever have chosen him. The love of God the Father gives us confidence, because he regards us as his child, a fellow heir with Christ. In God, "there is no fear in love; instead, perfect love drives out fear" (1 John 4:18).

When you feel like you're failing, when you can't hold it all together, or when you're not sure if you can ever be enough, cry out to your Abba Father. "Let us approach the throne of grace with boldness, so that we may receive mercy and find grace to help us in time of need" (Heb. 4:16).

An Anchor for the Soul

Shortly after her fifth birthday, my oldest daughter asked if she could pray to receive Christ as her Savior and Lord. I hesitated. I wondered if she would remember her moment of salvation. Would she remember the resurrection eggs; the conversation with her daddy after bedtime; or her simple, beautiful prayer of faith? I worried that in coming to faith at such a young age, she would lose assurance of her salvation later in life. To help capture her young, blossoming faith, I recorded a video of her sharing her testimony for her to watch when she may doubt.

This is a gift I would have loved to have had as a young girl, but I know a video can never be the final source of assurance for my daughter (or for me). My daughter doesn't need a video testimony to prove that her faith is real. She doesn't need the certificate from our church at her baptism or anything else to prove her right to come before God. By the blood of Christ, she can confidently enter the presence of God. On the days she sins, on the days she doubts, on the days she suffers, while this video may be a helpful reminder, it is not where her assurance ultimately lies.

Friend, your assurance doesn't lie in the approval of others. Your assurance doesn't lie in your own fickle emotions. Your assurance doesn't lie in any good works you could accomplish. No, your assurance, my assurance, and my daughter's assurance is a sure and steadfast anchor that has gone before us behind the curtain, removing any separation between us and God.[21] Our assurance is in the perfect, finished work of Christ.

No Conditions

Friend, there will always be people who reject you in this life because of your weaknesses and mistakes. You may miss out on a promotion, a friend might misunderstand you, a child may rebel against you, and a spouse may hurt you. However, God "will not leave you or abandon you" (Deut. 31:8).

There are no conditions for you to enter the presence of God. You don't have to prove anything to draw near to God. Has it been months since you've cracked open your Bible? Are

---

21. Hebrews 6:19

you feeling ashamed about lingering sin? Are you frustrated you can't keep it all together? Do you fear your heavenly Father will reject you because of your mistakes, your emotions, or your questions?

Know you can confidently enter the presence of God, not because you can prove you are good enough but because the blood of Jesus has made you more than enough. He has cleaned you; he has washed you.

> *Come boldly to the throne of grace,*
> *Ye wretched sinners come;*
> *And lay your load at Jesus' feet,*
> *And plead what He has done.*[22]

You can lay down the burden to be perfect and boldly approach God by the perfection of Christ. In his presence, there is fullness of joy.[23] In his presence, you can be confident of your wholeness in him.

When we have assurance that we can draw near to the throne of grace, we "have this hope as an anchor for the soul, firm and secure" (Heb. 6:19). And if we are confident in who we are in Christ, we can endure the storms of this life with enduring hope, holding fast to him.

---

22. Daniel Herbert, "Come Boldly to the Throne of Grace," 1838. Public domain.
23. Psalm 16:11

Remember

When you feel like God may not accept you because of your imperfections and sins, you can trade your shame and striving for the truth that:

I am enough because Christ gives me confidence before God the Father.

Reflect

1. Do you believe that Jesus not only loves you, but that he also likes you? Do you believe that God delights in you? Why or why not? How does your perception of his affection impact your spiritual life?

2. In the past, where have you found assurance in your faith? In your parents' beliefs, in your good works, in your church's programming, etc.? How can you surrender those false assurances and find true confidence in Christ?

3. What would it look like for you to draw near to God with full assurance? What idols, fears, and doubts are keeping you from enjoying God's presence fully?

Read

For further study, read 1 John 4:9–18. Praise God for his unconditional, sacrificial love for you. Ask that God would help you be confident in his love for you, so that you would not have any fear or shame in your relationship with him. Pray that he would show you ways you could love others like he has loved you.

Chapter 7
Enduring Hope

The nurse ushered my husband and me into the obstetrician's office after the technician finished the ultrasound. I knew something was wrong, since I was sitting on a soft couch rather than on the crinkling white paper of an examination table.

Only a minute later, the doctor entered, closed the door, and took a seat across from us. Her typical no-nonsense expression was now tempered with compassion. I reached for my husband's hand next to me.

"Unfortunately," she began, "we didn't find an embryo in the gestational sac." She leaned in toward us with her hands clasped in her lap. "I believe you've had an ectopic pregnancy. The baby never made it to your uterus. We now need to take measures to protect your health."

She continued to explain our options, but I didn't hear anything else. My husband asked her questions. I remained frozen on the couch, barely aware of their conversation. They scheduled a follow-up appointment, and my husband led me out of the office, down one elevator, up another, until we reached the parking deck.

"Are you sure you're okay to go home by yourself?" he asked me, and I nodded.

He left to go back to work, and I sat in my car alone. I pulled the week-old sonogram out of my purse—one with an arrow pointing to a perfect "O" and labeled, "gestational sac." They had told me everything was fine, not to worry about the bleeding, to come back in a week to confirm. For the past week, I had clung to the hope that this grainy black-and-white image overruled what I knew my body was telling me.

Now, that hope felt as empty as my womb.

"This isn't fair!" I yelled, finally releasing the hot tears and doubt I held inside me. "Why are you doing this to us, God?" I poured out my heart, but it felt as if my prayers weren't reaching beyond my car roof.

Only two months before, my husband and I had sat on another couch to receive bad news—this time from our adoption case worker. "I think it would be best if we put your home study process on hold for three months." Then, too, my husband held my hand as the tears poured down my cheeks.

We thought we had done everything right. When we began the adoption process, I stayed on top of the paperwork, sending in page after page of forms as soon as I could. Everything was moving quickly, until it wasn't. *Why God?* I had also asked then. *It's not fair.*

A few weeks later, I received a surprise positive pregnancy test on our anniversary trip, and I laughed to myself. *Oh, this must be why!* Of course, God knew we would need to pause the process since he planned to send us a biological child. For two weeks, I felt hope at the future again. We would simply start the adoption process again after this little one was born. I walked the streets of Washington, D.C., hand-in-hand with my husband, hopeful of our future.

Now, my anticipation of our growing family had been crushed. It seemed as if God was stripping away hope of another child, both by adoption and biologically. It felt like he was punishing me—I just couldn't figure out why.

Did I do something wrong to deserve this? I began wracking my brain. *Did I not care for my body well enough to hold this child? Did our past mistakes (and mistakes against us) mean we weren't fit to adopt a child? Was this God's discipline for me not being a good mother?* I looked at all I had done—all I had put my hope in—and it wasn't enough.

In this season of utter hopelessness, God exposed the shaky foundation of my hope and the more firm and secure hope he offered me instead.

More Than Wishful Thinking

As we processed our miscarriage, we had to inform our family who knew we had become pregnant. In addition to "I'm sorry," and "How can I help?" a few well-meaning family members tried to offer us hope: "This must mean something better is to come." "Maybe you'll be matched quickly for adoption." "I'm sure you'll be able to get pregnant again soon."

While I appreciated their sympathy, I also wanted to throw the phone across the room when I heard their unfounded positivity. I had planned out our family's growth perfectly, and look where that had gotten us. I had trusted in my hard work and blind optimism, and it had failed me. I had prayed for our future children, and yet my arms were empty.

Every morning for weeks, I dragged myself to my office armchair, set my closed Bible in my lap, and let the tears pour down my face. I asked God *why*. I listed all the "right" things I had done and wondered how I could have still ended up in this place. Day after day, I brought the complaints and my doubts. While the Holy Spirit comforted me in my grief, he also slowly softened my hardened heart and revealed the pride at the root of my bitterness. "Pride says, 'I don't deserve this,' or 'I know what's best for me and I would be better off if I were in control of my circumstances.'"[1]

As I worked through my grief, I was surprised to uncover entitlement beneath some of my pain. I didn't understand why bad things could happen to me when I had been so "good." I thought my own planning and striving could prevent hardship in my life. I wrongly believed any difficulty in my life was a means of punishment. I pridefully presumed I could ensure my own happy future.

Maybe you've felt this way too, in the trials of your life. In our self-sufficient Western culture, suffering is often seen as a sign of weakness or a result of failure.

> We live in a time when everyone's goal is to be perpetually healthy and constantly happy. If any one of us fails to live up to the standards that are advertised as normative, we are labeled as a problem to be solved, and a host of well-intentioned people rush to try out various cures on us. Or we are looked on as an enigma to be unraveled, in which case we are subjected to endless discussions, our lives examined

---

1. Kristen Wetherell and Sarah Walton, *Hope When It Hurts: Biblical Reflections to Help You Grasp God's Purpose in Your Suffering* (Epsom, United Kingdom: The Good Book Company, 2017), 102.

by researchers zealous for the clue that will account for our lack of health or happiness.[2]

This negative view of suffering has even crept into the church, with many believers being persuaded by a prosperity gospel. This false doctrine says if we believe and do the right things, we can avoid any adversity in this life. In this worldview, hope is limited to the expectation that we can create our own suffering-free future. If we are good enough, work hard enough, plan well enough, then we can be free from hardship. However, putting our hopes in our own efforts will always leave us doubting and despairing when trials inevitably arrive.

The prosperity gospel is antithetical to the gospel of Christ. Jesus promised his followers: "You *will* have suffering in this world." But he didn't leave us without hope: "Be courageous! I have conquered the world" (John 16:33, emphasis added). The cross-formed life doesn't *prevent* suffering. It provides us with hope and courage *through* suffering.

In the year after our miscarriage and delayed adoption, the Holy Spirit continued patiently to meet me in my grief and disbelief. Eventually, I was able to open my Bible again, and I asked God to give me something better than trusting in my

---

2. Eugene H. Peterson, *A Long Obedience in the Same Direction: Discipleship in an Instant Society,* 2nd ed. (Downers Grove, IL: InterVarsity Press, 2000), 138.

own efforts to secure my future. I pleaded with him for enduring hope to which I could cling.

I knew my true hope wasn't a silver lining. It wasn't wishful thinking. It wasn't even well-laid plans. So how could I find true hope that would make me feel whole again?

Holding onto Hope

There are several Hebrew words in the Old Testament translated to the English word *hope*. The one most frequently used is *tiqva*, which literally means "a cord" or a string.[3] Figuratively, it refers to an expectation or a thing that is longed for. It's something we hold onto. Its root word means "to wait."

As I searched the Scripture for hope, I found it interesting that the English word *hope* doesn't appear in the Old Testament until the book of Ruth. However, the Hebrew word for hope, *tiqva*, is used in one story before—one of my favorite stories— in the life of Rahab. This Canaanite prostitute played a surprising role in God's redemptive story, and her story gave me hope that I could find his redemption in my story too.

After delivering the Israelites out of Egypt, God commanded his people to conquer the Canaanite nations as they

---

3. James Strong, "tiqva," *Strong's Hebrew Lexicon (KJV)*, Blue Letter Bible, accessed December 2, 2023, https://www.blueletterbible.org/lexicon/h8615/kjv/wlc/0-1/.

took possession of the Promised Land God had given them.[4] In preparation, Joshua sent two spies to investigate Jericho, the first city they would face upon crossing the Jordan River. Evidently, they weren't very stealthy spies, because they were quickly found out by the king of Jericho. Rahab—a prostitute whose home was in the outer wall of Jericho—hid the Hebrew spies and lied to the king's guard to send them on a wild goose chase.[5]

It had been more than forty years since God's miraculous deliverance of Israel out of Egypt. Still the stories about the God of Israel's power circulated among the land of Canaan. Most Canaanites responded in fear or in pride,[6] but Rahab reacted differently. After hearing about the work of Yahweh, Rahab responded with faith and hope.

Rahab told the spies, "I know that the LORD has given you this land," (Josh. 2:9). She knew the power and purpose of Israel's God would not fail. So she pleaded with the spies according to Yahweh, God's covenant name with Israel: "Now please swear to me by the LORD that you will also show kindness to my father's family, because I showed kindness to you" (v. 12). The spies accepted her plea, and Rahab helped them escape. They told her to hang a scarlet cord—in Hebrew, a *tiqva*, the

---

4. Deuteronomy 31:3–5
5. Joshua 2:1–7
6. Joshua 2:10–11

same word as *hope*—from her window, and they would spare her and her family.[7] After Israel marched around Jericho seven days, God brought down the walls and wiped out the people—all except Rahab and her family.[8]

Rahab was willing to renounce everything—her home, her people, her profession—because she put her trust in the God of Israel. A single cord hanging from her window symbolized her hope in God. She clung to that single thread, to Yahweh, to a greater hope than anything in Jericho could offer her.

Who could have expected a Canaanite prostitute to be in the lineage of Christ[9] and to be commended for living by faith?[10] Who could have imagined such hope born out of hardship? Rahab's hope wasn't a full escape from suffering but hope through her suffering. The walls of Jericho still fell, and she had to rebuild her life among a new people, but she knew her only hope was in the true God of Israel.

Rahab's story helped me start loosening my grip on the hopes of this world. Rather than hold onto the rope of seemingly perfect plans and flawless efforts, I began reaching out for the true hope to which I must cling.

---

7. Joshua 2:14–21
8. Joshua 6:22–25
9. Matthew 1:5
10. Hebrews 11:31

Turning Our Minds to Hope

Even as I began to see God's hope in Scripture, specifically in Rahab's story, my grief often blinded me to the hope in my own story. I resonated with the prophet Jeremiah's lament of Israel's suffering. I, too, "continually remember [my affliction] and have become depressed" (Lam. 3:20). Nothing made sense, and all I wanted to do was weep.

In the book of Lamentations, Jeremiah wrote five chapters bursting with grief at the fall of Jerusalem. In the middle of his book, though, he interrupted his lament with a contrasting clause, "*But this I call to mind*, and therefore I have hope" (3:21 ESV, emphasis added). Amid his sorrow, Jeremiah reminded himself (and Israel) that this suffering is not all there is. He turned his mind, and therefore his heart, back to the hope of God.

"The steadfast love of the LORD never ceases; his mercies never come to an end; they are new every morning; great is your faithfulness. 'The LORD is my portion,' says my soul, 'therefore I will hope in him'" (vv. 22–24 ESV). Jeremiah chose to hope in God not *despite* his grief but *throughout* his grief. He refused to give up like so many of the Israelites had given up and given in to the world around them. He refused to put his hope in his own ability to free himself and his nation. Instead, he placed his confidence in the future promise of God to rescue and restore his people.

During seasons of suffering, we may feel anger, bitterness, confusion, and sorrow, and these emotions are not inherently bad. Our emotions act as a thermometer revealing the current temperature of our hearts. But we can never let our emotions be the thermostat of our lives—getting to set the standard for what is true.

No, like Jeremiah, when our hearts are roiling with emotions, we must repeatedly turn our minds away from our own fleeting efforts and emotions and toward the truth of our hope found in God—such as the truths we explored in the previous section of this book. We have enduring hope because we trust that the steadfast love, mercy, and faithfulness of God is always with us. We have enduring hope because we know our Creator loves us and made us in his image. We have enduring hope because we believe God is using this hardship to continue to perfect us and make us more like Christ.

After experiencing one of the hardships I feared the most—losing my baby in my womb—I was not left completely hopeless. I couldn't conjure up hope in myself or my situation, but God opened the eyes of my heart to my true confidence I had in him.

Confident Expectation

With every negative pregnancy test and adoption delay, I kept returning to my office armchair that year and to the stories of hope found in Scripture. As I flipped to the New Testament, I read that our hope put on flesh and dwelt among us.[11] Jesus—the hope of Rahab, Jeremiah, and all creation—now walked the earth. God's light shone into the darkness of my hopelessness, and my doubt and fear could not overcome it.[12]

The Greek word in the New Testament translated *hope* is *elpis*[13] or *elpizo*.[14] It is a confident expectation. It is not something we do; it is something we have. It comes from the root word *elpo*, which means to anticipate with pleasure. Eugene Peterson defines Christian hope as:

> Not spinning an illusion or fantasy to protect us from our boredom or our pain. It means a confident, alert expectation that God will do what he said he will do. It is imagination put in the harness of faith. It is a willingness to let God do it his way and in his time. It is the opposite of making plans that we demand that God put into effect, telling him both how and when to do it.[15]

---

11. John 1:14

12. John 1:4–5

13. Strong, "elpis," *Strong's Greek Lexicon (KJV)*, Blue Letter Bible, accessed December 2, 2023, https://www.blueletterbible.org/lexicon/g1680/kjv/tr/0-1/

14. Strong, "elpizo," *Strong's Greek Lexicon (KJV)*, Blue Letter Bible, accessed December 2, 2023, https://www.blueletterbible.org/lexicon/g1679/kjv/tr/0-1/

15. Peterson, *A Long Obedience in the Same Direction*, 144.

For so long, while I would have said I hoped in God, he was often my backup plan. My "plan A" was my own effort and knowledge. My confidence was in my adherence to the rules to ensure an outcome. My expectancy was in my meticulous blueprints for my life. I feared suffering because it was out of my control. I thought if I could be good enough, I would not have to walk through trials. My hope was in myself, not in God. So when my life seemed to fall apart, I realized how futile hoping in myself truly was.

The Confession of Our Hope

The author of Hebrews knew the temptation believers would feel to put their hope in themselves or in this world. His original audience was beginning to experience suffering and persecution, and rather than turning to Christ, they were relying on their own efforts to escape hardship. In view of Christ's faithful and perfect work, the author called them to surrender their strivings with a second "let us" exhortation: "*Let us* hold on to the confession of our hope without wavering, since he who promised is faithful" (Heb. 10:23, emphasis added).

The author of Hebrews had earlier defined our hope "as an anchor for the soul, firm and secure" (6:19). The anchor of our hope is Jesus, who went before us to secure a better future beyond anything we could have hoped. Our trust is not in our own strivings for perfect outcomes, but in our perfect High

Priest who introduces "a better hope . . . through which we draw near to God" (7:19).

Even in suffering, God desires his people to know the confidence and contentment they can have in him, so that we might "have strong encouragement to seize the hope set before us" (6:18). God sets his promises before us in his Word and invites us to hold fast to them as a boat holds fast to an anchor.

I've never sailed a boat (and it's been a decade since I've even ridden on one), but I do know what an anchor is. An anchor keeps a boat in place no matter how much it is tossed by the wind and waves. You may still experience choppy waters even if your anchor is secure, but the boat can only go so far. It may rock and pitch, but it will not be carried away.

When we hold fast to our hope in Christ, we will still experience the wind and waves of hardship in this life. Our suffering may shake us, but it cannot destroy us. Our plans may fail, people might reject us, and we may face our greatest fears. Even in these storms, we can maintain a sureness and steadfastness, trusting Christ himself keeps us from floating away or going under.

This is not a hope we have to work for or find in ourselves or in this world. It is set before us in the perfect person and work of Christ.

He Is Faithful

What happens, then, when we don't hold onto this hope? Hebrews 10:23 calls us to hold on "without wavering," but in my doubt, fear, and grief, I have wavered. I have pushed God away, questioned him, and shook my fist at him. I have become so blinded by my suffering that I could not see the hope set before me. I have become so numb by sorrow that I could not feel the rope connected to my firm and secure anchor. In the middle of life's storms, I have felt like I was drifting away or, worse, drowning altogether.

However, in his grace and kindness, God held me fast. All the time I thought I had been holding my life together, he was the one keeping me firm and secure. I thought Jesus had been sleeping during tempests in my life. He was there all along—waiting for me to call out to him so he could speak, "Peace! Be still!" over the gales rocking my life (Mark 4:39 ESV). While I had been clinging onto my doubt, fear, and grief, Christ had still been holding onto me. And, friend, he is holding on to you too.

There will be days we lose hope. We will strive to make ourselves firm and secure. We will cling to the empty promises of this world. We will put our trust in others' approval, in work accomplishments, and even in our own religious performance. We will build our house on the shifting sands of self-sufficient optimism. And our kingdoms will fall.

Even in that, God has not left us without hope.

When we lose our hope in Christ, we can trust that hope himself is hanging onto us. In terms of nautical science, the anchor and boat equally hold on to each other. However, in the Christian life, it's the anchor that ultimately keeps us secure. When our weakness, sin, and doubt lead us to loosen our grip on Christ our anchor, he still holds fast to us: "if we are faithless, he remains faithful" (2 Tim. 2:13). Our hope is not in our own perfect devotion. Our hope is anchored in Christ's perfect faithfulness to us.

He who set our hope before us will also carry us until the end—until our hope is ultimately fulfilled.

Our Ultimate Hope

Since that difficult year, we have brought two children into our family—one biologically and one through adoption. I praise the Lord every day for these two precious children, but I must remember they are not the fulfillment of my hope. My children are good and beautiful gifts from a generous and gracious God, but they can never give me hope. Neither can the material possessions, ministry opportunities, or physical health God blesses me with here on earth.

More than these temporal gifts, God "has given us new birth into a living hope through the resurrection of Jesus Christ" (1 Pet. 1:3). All the world's blind optimism and self-sufficient manifestations will pass away. But God has promised us a better "inheritance that is imperishable, undefiled, and unfading, kept in heaven for you" (v. 4). Our ultimate hope is not the perfectly happy and healthy life we can achieve in our own strength here on earth, but in an eternal reward earned, guaranteed, and guarded by Christ himself.

This future hope is how we can rejoice when we "suffer grief in various trials" (v. 6). We don't fight to control our suffering but can trust that God is using our hardship to draw us closer to him. "We do not have to live our lives anxiously toiling and striving to control the circumstances around us. Trust Christ, and know that every aspect of our lives is purposefully designed to make us more like him and bring glory to his name."[16] Suffering isn't an obstacle to the "perfected" life. It is a necessary means by which Christ is at work perfecting us. James says we can "consider it a great joy . . . whenever you experience various trials" because we know suffering will make us "mature and complete, lacking nothing" (James 1:2, 4). We need not fear when suffering derails our plans and dreams, because God has guaranteed a better hope to come.

Friends, nothing on this earth can offer you comfort and confidence when you groan under suffering. From a career disappointment to a cancer diagnosis—our grief reminds us that

---

16. Wetherell and Walton, *Hope When It Hurts*, 38.

the fulfillment of our hope is yet to come. The hope of God doesn't say, "You'll get that promotion next year," or, "I promise to heal every disease on earth." Our hope sits at the right hand of the throne of God, promising that God is working together all this suffering for our good and God's glory to make us more like him.[17]

This Hope Will Not Disappoint

In writing this chapter, I returned to my prayer journals from that dark year of my life. A few months after our miscarriage, I wrote:

God, how many times do I try to pull myself up by my bootstraps instead of falling on my face in surrender? My natural response is to work instead of to wait. God, help me to stop trying to control my future and instead trust in your plan. I can rest in you! God, you have not left me alone in this hard life. Even if the worst-case scenario happened, you would still be there. I could never lose you; and that is enough.

I wrote these words with tears of sorrow, but I read them now with tears of joy. I'm overwhelmed by how God carried me

---

17. Romans 8:28–29

through that season. I had thought I was pulling myself out of my grief. Looking back, though, I can see the strong and tender hands of God were around me, lifting me up and giving me hope.

Though I would say our delayed adoption and miscarriage was one of the most poignant seasons of suffering in our life, I faced trials before and since then as well—difficult medical diagnoses, relational strain, a global pandemic, severe anxiety. Every time life doesn't go the way I plan, I'm tempted to turn inward—to figure it out and control it in my own self-sufficient strength and knowledge.

By the grace and power of the Holy Spirit within me, I'm learning to seize the hope God has set before me. I'm learning to lay down my strivings to earn my own perfect future and, instead, to rest assured in the future hope Christ has prepared for me. I'm learning to release the shame of my suffering and trust that God is using this for my good and his glory. Over and again, I'm finding this "hope will not disappoint us, because God's love has been poured out in our hearts through the Holy Spirit who was given to us" (Rom. 5:5). The living hope God offers me is better than any future I could create on my own.

The Hope of His Calling

Where does your hope lie today? Are you placing your security in your ability to plan, to make money, to work hard enough for a certain future? Are you saying you trust in God's purpose for your life, but saving it as a "backup" plan? I have learned the hard way, you cannot put your hope in both God and this world.

God has set a better hope before you. You don't have to strive to ensure a positive outcome. You don't have to worry one wrong step will ruin your plans. You don't have to build your own foundation. The burden to create a hope and a future was never on your shoulders. Jesus has offered himself as your anchor, the one who keeps you safe and secure during life's storms. Jesus has promised you a better future, and he has guaranteed to keep you until the end.

When you feel like your own failures and mistakes have left you hopeless, "I pray that the eyes of your heart may be enlightened so that you may know what is the hope of his calling" (Eph. 1:18). I pray you would remember the wealth of God's glorious inheritance in us—that he will always be faithful to his promises toward his children. I pray you would rest in the immeasurable greatness of his power—that he raised Christ from the dead, conquered death, and created a place for us in heaven.[18] Our hope is not wishful thinking or positive affirmations. Our hope is a joyful, confident expectation that Jesus Christ will always fulfill God's promises toward us.

---

18. Ephesians 1:18–23

Once our lives are built on the solid rock of our hope in Christ, he invites us to walk forward in faith. "Hoping does not mean doing nothing. . . . It means going about our assigned tasks, confident that God will provide the meaning and the conclusions."[19] Looking forward to the hope of eternity does not negate faithfulness in the present. When our hope is in Christ's sufficiency and not our own, we can trust and obey him in every season of life.

As we draw near in boldness to God and hold fast to our enduring hope in him, we will find ourselves empowered to walk forward in his love and the good works he has prepared for us.

 ## Remember

When you feel hopeless as you endure sufferings and trials, you can trade your shame and striving for the truth that:

I am enough because my hope is secure in Christ.

 ## Reflect

1. What are you tempted to put your hope in—your knowledge and control, your good works, your financial

---

19. Peterson, *A Long Obedience in the Same Direction*, 144.

security, etc.? Can you confess the false hopes in your heart to God?

2. Are you currently enduring suffering? Like Jeremiah, how can you turn your heart and mind to hope when everything feels hopeless?

3. What does it look like to hold onto Christ during hard seasons? How can you also rest knowing that he is holding onto you?

 ## Read

For further study, read 2 Corinthians 4:16–18. Write down the temporal things you have put your hope in. Then praise God for his promise of an eternal weight of glory. Lament the suffering and trials in your life and ask God to lift your eyes from these momentary afflictions to the enduring hope found in Christ.

Chapter 8

Love-Motivated Good Works

Are you still watching? The television screen taunted me.

I had lost track of how long I had been sitting on our couch. My six-month-old daughter lay asleep in my arms. Remnants of her projectile spit-up stained my sweatshirt. My unwashed hair was slicked back into a greasy ponytail. My second—no, third—cup of lukewarm coffee sat on the table next to me. I couldn't tell if the sour smell came from my daughter or me, or both of us. I looked up at the overflowing laundry basket next to me and glanced behind to the mound of dishes on the kitchen counter. I knew I *should* do something, but everything was just so overwhelming.

I picked up the remote and clicked "yes" to keep watching Netflix.

The past year had been a whirlwind. We had our first baby, and my mom was diagnosed with cancer. My husband graduated from his master's program and accepted his first job. I quit my job and became a stay-at-home mom. We moved across the state with a newborn. A leak caused water damage the first night in our new home, and for weeks I couldn't unpack the towers of boxes while the flooring was replaced.

Everything was out of control—out of *my* control. Try as I might, I couldn't seem to do anything right. And since I couldn't do it all perfectly, I subconsciously decided I wouldn't even try at all.

In my postpartum fog, I spent my days caring for my daughter's basic needs before falling back onto the couch to watch another show. I drowned my anxieties in chips and salsa and gallons of cookie dough ice cream. I went through the motions at church but didn't bother to spend time with God during the week. I indulged in books and shows I knew weren't good for my heart and mind. I scrolled social media for hours—comparison swinging me between pride and envy. I lashed out at my husband for being able to leave the house and be "productive." All I had was an endless cycle of diapers, laundry, and dishes shining a spotlight on all my imperfections.

I now know the months following the birth or adoption of a child are acutely stressful, and some of my anxiety and depression were a result of unbalanced hormones. I also recognize my lack of growth in that season was not just due to physiological stressors but to my prideful perfectionism. For years, I had boasted in the work of my hands—what I could do to prove I was enough. When it was all stripped away, I didn't know who I was anymore.

I had begun to experience freedom from perfectionism before I became a mother, but that tumultuous season swung me to the other extreme into licentiousness—not caring about keeping God's commands or trying to do better at all. Since I knew I couldn't obey God's Word perfectly on my own, I gave up trying to follow it altogether.

At the time, it felt easier to sit in stained leggings, to watch one more show, and to eat another bag of chips. However, I found it didn't give me more satisfaction than anxiously striving to be and do better. I had believed giving up all efforts of goodness and taking away any expectations would make me feel whole again. Instead, I despaired more over my imperfections. Rather than finding freedom, I lingered in a period of dark depression, wondering if my shoddy state was the best I could ever be.

Looking for Freedom in Imperfection

My hopelessness during this season of weakness is not an unusual one. Many influencers I followed on Instagram—even Christian ones—invited their followers to lay aside all expectations and embrace our flaws. The motherhood culture I found online exalted the "hot mess mama." It celebrated loose buns, dirty sweatshirts, full kitchen sinks, and reliance on coffee during the day and wine at night. Outside of motherhood, this kind of cultural mindset instructs us not to strive for anything more than these imperfections. Even as Christians, we're often told to focus on how God "gives greater grace" (James 4:6) and to not worry so much about our growth in holiness. God doesn't want us to strive, so why try at all? While this reasoning masquerades as the gospel of grace, it ultimately leaves us empty and without hope for the future. Perfection can never satisfy us, but neither can our imperfections. So how can we find wholeness without idolizing our perfection or our imperfections?

Jen Wilkin has called this response to our inadequacies "'celebratory failurism'—the idea that believers cannot obey the Law and will fail at every attempt. Furthermore, our failure is ultimately cause to celebrate because it makes grace all the more beautiful."[1] In this perspective, all we can do is accept that we are sinners and not burden ourselves by trying to do better. Any call to growth or self-discipline is too oppressive, and we should deride anyone who puts on a clean pair of jeans and attempts to cross something off a list.

Believing we can earn God's favor through obeying his law (legalism) is based in fear and shame. But disregarding his law (license) is also grounded in fear and shame. If I'm afraid I'll

---

1. Jen Wilkin, "Failure Is Not a Virtue," *The Gospel Coalition*, May 1, 2014, https://www.thegospelcoalition.org/article/failure-is-not-a-virtue/.

never overcome my sinful desires, I will stop trying to fight my hot temper, my sharp tongue, and my lustful thoughts. If I'm ashamed of my lingering sins, I'll attempt to cover them up with false bravado and boast in my "freedom" from rules.

"Our work goes wrong . . . both when we work anxiously and when we don't work at all, when we become frantic and compulsive in our work and when we become indolent and lethargic in our work."[2] Neither anxious toil nor fearful lethargy could give me the freedom for which I longed.

Maybe you, too, have fallen into lethargy out of desire to escape perfectionist expectations. Maybe you've given up because the career goal, the flawless appearance, or the desired relationships you worked hard for slipped through your grasping fingers. Friend, the good news is that there is a third option. Unlike legalism or licentiousness, true obedience flourishes out of love. When we are united with Christ, the point is not about what rules we do or do not follow, "what matters is faith working through love" (Gal. 5:6). So how, then, does our love work?

Saved for Love and Good Works

Thus far in our reading of Hebrews, the author has focused on the supremacy of Christ. Our satisfaction and sufficiency are

2. Eugene H. Peterson, *A Long Obedience in the Same Direction: Discipleship in an Instant Society*, 2nd ed. (Downers Grove, IL: InterVarsity Press, 2000), 109.

not found in anything that we could do but in Christ's perfect work he has accomplished for us and is still doing inside of us. Our assurance and hope come from him alone.

After pages instructing us to not earn our salvation, the author of Hebrews offers a third "let us" statement, with a seemingly surprising application: "*Let us* consider one another in order to provoke love and good works" (Heb. 10:24, emphasis added). The author spent chapters telling us our goodness will never be enough, then he instructs us to do good things. This appears to be a contradiction to his message. Why should we attempt to do good—and encourage others to do the same—if our goodness can never save us?

The connection between Christ's perfect sacrifice and our imperfect efforts lies in the word *love*. When we believe our labors are the basis of our salvation, our efforts are motivated by fear and shame. We will oscillate between legalism or license. However, when our good works are based in Christ's finished work of salvation, they are motivated by love. And "perfect love drives out fear" (1 John 4:18).

In his grace, God saves us before he calls us to obey.[3] He sets us apart before instructing us to live set apart.[4] Christ became our righteousness before inviting us to walk righteously.[5] God

---

3. Titus 2:11–14
4. 1 Peter 2:9–10
5. 2 Corinthians 5:21–6:1

does not require our good work before he redeems us.[6] But he also does not leave us in our sin after forgiving us.[7]

How we view the relationship between our love and good works will determine whether we obey God out of duty or delight.

How Love Inspires Good Work

My favorite Bible verse as a teenager was Romans 12:1: "Therefore, brothers and sisters, in view of the mercies of God, I urge you to present your bodies as a living sacrifice, holy and pleasing to God; this is your true worship." While my peers chose Bible verses about God granting them the desires of their heart[8] and giving them strength to do all things,[9] I pretentiously chose a verse about what I could do for God. I would be a living sacrifice, striving to make myself set apart and to be acceptable to him. I saw my true worship as all the good things I could do *for* God.

I misunderstood the verse's greater context. Romans 12:1 begins with "therefore," harkening back to the first part of the letter. Paul pens this call to sacrificial living after chapters of rich exposition about God's merciful plan of salvation. My

---

6. Romans 5:8
7. John 8:11
8. Psalm 37:4
9. Philippians 4:13

good work was to be done "in view of the mercies of God" (v. 1). Instead, I presented my body as a living sacrifice *in view of my own sufficiency*. And I learned the hard way that those self-sufficient sacrifices could never make me whole.

After the eyes of our hearts have been opened to how deep God's love is for us, we cannot help but offer ourselves as a sacrifice back to him. Only love for God leads to the true worship of sacrificial living—not as a way to earn God's mercy, but as a way to joyfully live in response to his mercy.

How Good Works Reveal Love

Jesus came to free us from the burden to save ourselves through obedience to the law, and he also called those he saved to obey his law. The night before he offered his life as the final sacrifice for sin, Jesus told his followers, "If you keep my commands you will remain in my love, just as I have kept my Father's commands and remain in his love" (John 15:10). His sacrifice wouldn't negate his followers' obedience. It would empower them to walk in greater obedience.

As Christians, we are no longer under the law. Still, the law now lives in us. "Do we then nullify the law through faith? Absolutely not! On the contrary, we uphold the law" (Rom. 3:31). We don't put our faith in our adherence to God's commands. Neither do we forsake God's commands completely. The law shows us what Christ is like—and how we can be like him. Our love for Christ should always overflow into obedience to Christ.

If we truly believe the glorious truths about who God is, who we are, and how he is saving us, then our lives will look different. "The one who says, 'I have come to know him,' and yet doesn't keep his commands, is a liar, and the truth is not in him. But whoever keeps his word, truly in him the love of God is made complete" (1 John 2:4–5). God's work of love is made complete—and we are made whole—through our love for and obedience to him.

He Has Given Us Everything We Need

I began typing the first words of this chapter on New Year's Day. Knowing my propensity to hope in how much I can change myself, I'm hesitant now to make grand resolutions and strict routines. I fear falling back into my perfectionist strivings, but I also don't want to remain stagnant in my life and faith.

This year, I felt the Holy Spirit revealing certain areas of my life where I needed to grow in Christlikeness. It wasn't a call to labor for perfection. Neither was it an excuse to wallow in imperfections. The Spirit was inviting me to take up my cross and follow Christ by radically obeying him.

On the outside, radical obedience and perfectionism look similar: a commitment to pursuing our work with excellence. On the inside, though, the motivations are wildly different. Perfectionism seeks to please man, but radical obedience seeks to please God. Perfectionism is rooted in anxiety, frustration, and endless striving. Radical obedience is rooted in peace, joy, and endless surrender. Perfectionism chokes, paralyzes, and prevents us from even starting. Radical obedience launches, spurs, and propels us forward.[10]

I sat with a blank notebook in my lap and asked God, "Am I seeking my own glory? Or am I seeking lavish, extravagant fulfillment of what [you] asked of me?"[11] As God began to reveal the good works he had prepared for me this year,[12] I wondered how I could keep myself from swinging to the extremes of legalism and license. How could I end the year more like Christ—not burnt out from striving or ashamed from failing?

Then I laughed to myself. I realized I needed to be reminded (again) of the gospel truths I was exploring in this book. God wasn't handing me an assignment, expecting me to figure out how to do love-motivated good works on my own. He was

---

10. Ashlee Gadd, *Create Anyway: The Joy of Pursuing Creativity in the Margins of Motherhood* (Minneapolis, MN: Bethany House, 2023), 113.
11. Gadd, *Create Anyway*, 114.
12. Ephesians 2:10

inviting me to live according to his perfect power already working within me.

God reminded me, "His divine power has given us everything required for life and godliness" (2 Pet. 1:3). He has already provided me with everything I need in him to grow more like Christ today. And tomorrow, God will give me exactly what I need to obey him—and the day after that, and the day after that.

Like the Israelites relied on him for their daily portion of manna in the wilderness,[13] our love-motivated good work must rely on God to provide us the strength, wisdom, endurance, and love to obey his commands. And just as the Israelites had to step out of their tents and gather God's miraculous provision, so we also have the choice to step out in faith and walk in the good works God has prepared for us.

When we do, our good works will be empowered by God, prompted by his promises, grown over time, and repeatedly informed by the truth.

Empowered by God

Looking at the good works to which God has called me, I often wonder, *How am I ever going to do this? How am I going to faithfully shepherd my discipleship group? How am I going to train*

---

13. Exodus 16

up my children in gospel truth? How am I going to write in a way that honors God and serves my readers?

Peter clearly answers my question of how I can live a life of godliness: By "the knowledge of him who called us by his own glory and goodness" (2 Pet. 1:3). I am empowered by God when I focus on his strength made perfect in my weaknesses.[14] The more I meditate on the infinite glory and goodness of God—not fixating on my own finite glory and goodness—the more I will be spurred on to love and good works. Yes, I will work hard, but I do so trusting God is working in me.[15] The more I know God, the more I will become like him and fulfill his purpose in me.

The good things I can do will amount to nothing unless I am relying on God's strength. The psalmist reminds us of the futility of trying to strive in our own efforts: "Unless the LORD builds a house, its builders labor over it in vain" (Ps. 127:1). We don't do good things to prove ourselves, to empower ourselves, or to establish the work of our own hands. No, we do good work because God is already at work in us.

Prompted by Promises

In the late afternoon, when I ask my children to clean up their toys, I will often be met with grumbling and sluggishness. I must remind them what is on the other side of their

---

14. 2 Corinthians 12:9
15. Philippians 2:12–13; Colossians 1:29

obedience: "If you get your toys picked up quickly, you'll have time to watch a show before dinner." Soon, they're hastily tossing Magna-Tiles into bins, dolls in the crib, and plastic food into the play kitchen. Their obedience is driven by a promise (for them, an episode of *Wild Kratts*).

Our obedience, too, is prompted by promises. "By these [God] has given us very great and precious promises, so that through them you may share in the divine nature, escaping the corruption that is in the world because of evil desire" (2 Pet. 1:4). The reward for our good works is not just in heaven. By walking in obedience, we grow closer to him and become more like him here on earth. While we will never reach full perfection in these bodies, God promises that we can and will become more perfect as he is perfect.[16]

Doing whatever we desire may seem like freedom, but it's bondage to our sinful flesh.[17] God promises us true freedom through our obedience to him—sanctification for now and glorification forever.[18] While God does not guarantee our obedience will lead to worldly success, he does promise that our faithfulness will allow us to receive his blessings: "All these blessings will come and overtake you, because you obey the LORD your God" (Deut. 28:2).

---

16. Matthew 5:48
17. Romans 6:16
18. Romans 6:22

When our good works are motivated by fear of failing or the shame of losing favor, we will burn out or give up. But when our good works are prompted by God's promise of fruitfulness in our lives, we can obey out of joy.

Grown Over Time

I'm not a very patient person. After one workout, I would like to see bicep definition. After my first attempt, I would like perfectly baked bread. After one prayer, I wish all my sinful struggles would go away. Realistically, none of these changes can happen overnight.

God is patient with our spiritual growth, often described as a "walk" in Scripture.[19] Our Christian life is not a destination we reach here on earth but the ongoing journey we take by the Spirit in us. We grow in our Christlikeness by putting one foot in front of the other again and again to become more like him.

Because of the promises set before us, Peter encourages us to "make every effort to supplement your faith with goodness, goodness with knowledge, knowledge with self-control, self-control with endurance, endurance with godliness, godliness with brotherly affection, and brotherly affection with love" (2 Pet. 1:5–7). Peter isn't giving us a step-by-step list to check off. He's exhorting us to continual growth by "possess[ing]

---

19. Romans 8:4; Galatians 5:16

these qualities in increasing measure" (v. 8). These are characteristics we will grow in a little more day after day. While we may be stronger in one than another, we will not fully master any of them until we reach eternity.

That's okay. "God does not expect our good work to be flawless in order for them to be good. . . . God is pleased through Christ to accept our sincere obedience, although it contains many weaknesses and imperfections."[20] The point of our good works is not overnight perfection but depending more on Christ and becoming more like him every day.

Informed by Truth

I would love to say that after God revealed the root of my striving, from then on, I walked in God-empowered, promised-prompted, Spirit-led growth. Really, it's a lesson I'm constantly learning. Self-sufficient perfectionism and love-motivated good works can appear the same on the outside, so I'm constantly examining my heart to get to the root of my obedience. I must be reminded of Christ's good work in me—and maybe you do too.

Peter knew his readers would wrestle with spiritual growth for the rest of their Christian lives on earth—either with anxious striving or ashamed despair. After instructing them in how

---

20. Kevin DeYoung, *The Hole in Our Holiness: Filling the Gap between Gospel Passion and the Pursuit of Godliness* (Wheaton, IL: Crossway, 2012), 67.

to grow in their faith, he gives three reminders: "I will always remind you about these things." "I think it is right . . . to wake you up with a reminder." "And I will also make every effort so that you are able to recall these things" (2 Pet. 1:12–13, 15). Peter made it his life's purpose to remind the church of the "great and precious promises" they had in Christ (v. 4).

I need these reminders every day. From the moment I wake up, I'm barraged with messages on my phone telling me to do more. I must put down my phone and pick up God's Word to fight the lies with truth. My flesh tempts me to take control or to give up when my day gets overwhelming. I must cast all my anxieties on God, trusting he cares more about my growth than I do.[21] When I'm burdened by the expectations of others, I can lay them at the feet of Jesus and take the easy load he offers me.[22]

On that New Year's Day, when I looked through the hopes and goals I believed the Holy Spirit was leading me to, I was excited not burdened. I looked forward to stepping into the plans God had set before me, because I was confident that "he who started a good work in [me would] carry it on to completion until the day of Christ Jesus" (Phil. 1:6).

21. 1 Peter 5:7
22. Matthew 11:28–30

Undeserved Rest

I used to hate taking bubble baths. Maybe it was the years living in a dorm room with a shared bathroom followed by an apartment with a less than desirable tub. A hot, bubbly soak was just never on my list of relaxing activities. Even when my husband and I moved into our first home with a large tub in the master bathroom, it remained empty except for toddler bath toys and dirty towels until midway through my second pregnancy.

My pelvic floor pain had become unbearable, so my husband drew me a bath and poured in Epsom salts. Still wary of the idea, I tentatively lowered myself into the warm water and looked up at the ceiling. While my body instantly relaxed, my mind raced and my hands fidgeted. I felt guilty sitting there doing nothing but soaking in the aromatic oils and salts. My fingers had just begun to prune when I realized the true reason why I don't enjoy bubble baths.

They aren't productive.

Unable to do anything except pop bubbles, I felt the itch to do *something* to earn this rest. I began making a list of ways to return my husband's favor, to make up for the time lost sitting here, to make this relaxation worth it.

This belief that I need to earn my rest isn't limited to bubble baths. I often think I must justify my spiritual rest through my good works; I sign up for another volunteer opportunity at church, purchase another Bible curriculum to do with my kids, and make a habit tracker of neglected spiritual disciplines. Only if I do enough of these good things, I believe, can I merit the rest of God. Instead of resting in the finished work of Christ, I spin my wheels trying to prove I am worthy of his rest.

God's Free Gift of Rest

Friend, we do not have to complete a list of good works to earn our rest. Rest is a gracious gift from a limitless God to his limited creation. After freeing the Israelites from Egyptian slavery, God inscribed into stone the importance of rest for his people and provided two reasons why they should rest. Exodus 20:11 says we rest because we trust God as our Creator. God modeled for us the importance of both work and rest in his act of creation. Deuteronomy 5:15 commands us to rest because we trust God as our Savior. We know there is no amount of work we can do to save ourselves. We are fully dependent on him.

God's gift of rest isn't merely about taking a break. It's an integral part of our love-motivated good works.

Sometimes the good work to which God is calling you is not to do *more* but to do *less*. When you know your value isn't dependent on what you produce, you can rest without anxiety or guilt. Rest is not the reward for your good work. It's part of your good work. It's intentionally setting down the labor of your hands and believing that only God can establish it.[23]

If your efforts are motivated by your love for God and his love for you, you don't fear the uncompleted task lists, unanswered emails, and endless baskets of laundry. You can embrace God's gracious cycle of work and rest, trusting Christ's perfection has secured your ultimate rest in him.

Not Meant to Work Alone

You may be in a weary season, having lost all hope that you could change *at all*. Or you may be in a season of striving, trusting in your own effort to change *it all*. Neither way brings you closer to the perfection you have in Christ.

If you're feeling burdened by expectations to be perfect, the goal is not to throw off any rules and growth altogether. The goal is not to focus even harder on how you will do better. You can only grow in your Christlikeness by releasing your self-sufficient expectations and focusing more on God's faithful love. Even when you fail, you don't have to fear, because you are not alone in the Christian life. Jesus "is more committed to your growth in him than you are."[24]

---

23. Psalm 90:17
24. Dane C. Ortlund, *Deeper: Real Change for Real Sinners* (Wheaton, IL: Crossway, 2021), 31.

The Spirit of Christ is working in you today. He's showering you with grace when you are burdened by legalism. He's exhorting you to godliness when you fall into license. He's reminding you of God's love for you and the good work he's prepared for you. We are never working alone.

God has put the Spirit of Christ inside of us, but he's also given us an equally powerful gift, his church—the body of Christ around us.

Stir Up One Another

What led me out of that dark postpartum season was not more "self-care" time spent watching another show, taking a bath, or escaping my responsibilities. It wasn't a greater resolve to pull myself out of my mess and misery. It wasn't even my hormones slowly rebalancing.

No, what led me out was an older sister in Christ pushing me to love and good works. She encouraged me to get back into God's Word, even if it was only for minutes a day. She prayed for and with me. She invited me deeper into Christian community. She called me out on my sin and helped me fight it by the power of the Spirit.

Slowly, I felt light breaking through. The spiritual disciplines that used to be a burden were now a delight. The "rules" I was running from were actually what brought me freedom. As I meditated on God's sufficient goodness and faithful love rather than my own insufficiencies and faithlessness, I felt empowered to walk in obedience.

The writer of Hebrews didn't only call us to love and good works, he called us to "stir up one another" to do the same (Heb. 10:24 ESV). Our growth in godliness is never meant to be done in a vacuum. In every season of weariness, God has sent me sisters and brothers in Christ to draw me back to himself. They remind me of the steadfast love of God, my limitations as a human, and the perfect work of Christ in me. They strengthen my assurance of faith and help me hold onto hope. They encourage me to love and obey God more. Every truth in this book is one that I've learned alongside other brothers and sisters in Christ.

Christian community is never perfect because we as individual Christians are not perfect. Together, though, we encourage one another to hope in the perfect work of Christ on our behalf. When we learn to lay down our efforts to be perfect on our own, we can wholly lean into this God-given community vulnerably and unashamed.

 Remember

When you feel burdened by God's commands, you can trade your shame and striving for the truth that:

I am enough because God's love empowers my good work.

Reflect

1. How have you struggled with "celebratory failurism" in the past—believing that you can never succeed, so you shouldn't even try? In what ways has this perspective still left you unsatisfied?

2. What would it look like for you to rely on God's strength—not your own efforts—to walk in obedience?

3. Are you following God's command to rest? Why or why not? How can you incorporate rhythms of rest into your day and week?

 Read

For further study, read 2 Peter 1:5–7. You read these verses in this chapter, but now pray and ask God to reveal which area you need to grow in. Once the Holy Spirit convicts your heart on an area of growth, look for other Bible verses related to that topic. Meditate on those verses, pray for God to strengthen you, and seek to walk forward in obedience.

Chapter 9
Biblical Community

My college suitemate stood at the door of my dorm room. She held out her arms, pleading, "You always pretend like you're perfect, Bethany!" She yelled, loud enough for our third suitemate to stick her head into the hall and check on the commotion. "You expect me to tell you all the hard stuff going on in my life, while you pretend like nothing is going wrong in yours. I know that can't be true."

I sat on my twin bed staring at my best friend, wondering what to say—what I could say. We both knew she was right and were wondering if I would finally be able to open up to her. "I do have problems," I whimpered back. "I just don't like to talk about them."

My suitemate snorted. "How am I supposed to trust you with my problems if you don't trust me with yours?"

Her accusation hung thick in the stale dormitory air. We stared at each other in silence. I hugged my hot-pink pillow closer to my chest and refused to meet her gaze. When it became obvious that I didn't have an answer, she turned on her heels and marched down the narrow hallway. She slammed her door, a resounding end to our friendship.

Since our first semester of college, we had coordinated our class schedules, spent hours scrolling bridesmaids' dresses on Pinterest, and gone out for late-night slushies during exam week. Yet I could never divulge the hardest, darkest parts of my heart.

I couldn't tell her I felt like an imposter most of the time. I was weighed down with overwhelming pressure to finish college with a 4.0 GPA. I struggled with purity in my relationship with my boyfriend. I stretched myself across three jobs, worried how I would pay the next month's bills. I agonized over post-graduate opportunities, still unsure what I was supposed to do with my life. The hardest part of all, I felt like I had to hide these struggles and more, or else I would let others down.

My best friend and suitemate said she wanted to know my problems. I feared once she did, she wouldn't want to know me anymore.

My college suitemate wasn't the first "close" friend I had held at arm's length—afraid if they got too close, the cracks in my façade might show. My classmates in high school probably thought I was a judgmental prude. My college peers likely saw me as a self-righteous know-it-all. Even as I stepped into adulthood, I kept my new coworkers and friends at a distance, creating the persona of a perfect wife, employee, and church member.

I craved friendship, but I feared authentic community. I was terrified of anyone knowing who I truly was. The more insufficient and dissatisfied with my life I felt, the more I pulled away from others—especially within the church.

Even when I began discovering God's compassion and grace toward my imperfections, I wasn't sure other believers would show me the same kind of grace. I was learning God was slow to anger, but I still believed the church would be quick to reject me because of my sin and struggles. As God started to open my heart to his unconditional love toward me, I didn't yet trust his people could love me in the same way.

Maybe you feel this same wariness around the people of God. You wonder how you can enjoy biblical community when you fear they won't accept you—imperfections and all.

Naked and Unashamed

Our longing for community is engrained into our DNA. We were made in the image of a relational, triune God. Our Creator declared, "It is not good for the man to be alone" (Gen. 2:18). Before Adam and Eve ate the forbidden fruit, they enjoyed perfect fellowship with God and each other: "Both the man and his wife were naked, yet felt no shame" (v. 25). After they disobeyed, sin fractured humanity's relationships with

God and with other image-bearers: "The eyes of both of them were opened, and they knew they were naked; so they sewed fig leaves together and made coverings for themselves" (3:7).

For the first time, Adam and Eve saw their imperfections and wanted to hide themselves from God and one another. When God sought them out, already knowing what they had done, they deflected their sin and blamed others. They tried to preserve their innocence by betraying someone (or something) else. They tried to live a life independent from God and each other.

From then on, a person's sin impacted not only one's own life but also the lives of those around them. Humanity's self-centered pursuit of satisfaction and sufficiency led to pride, idolatry, sexual immorality, and murder. When people no longer found their identity in their Creator, they sought to build up their own image at the expense of others. Our capacity for true community was crushed by the weight of our sin.

If we feel like we must prove we are enough in and of ourselves, we will spurn the help of others. In our striving for independence, we will envy, tear down, and resent others. In our shame, we will blame, deceive, and disconnect from others. We will champion individualism and self-reliance because anything less would require admitting our insecurities and insufficiencies to each other. We can't be honest with others because they might take advantage of our vulnerabilities.

So, like our first parents, we sew together fig leaves to hide our sin and shame.

Saved into an Imperfect Family

Unfortunately, within the church, we also can seek to hide our true selves in the presence of our sisters and brothers in Christ. We claim to be a community of sinners saved by grace, yet we sometimes pretend our goodness results from our own efforts. We chat with each other on Sunday mornings—responding to each "How are you?" with "I'm good!" To admit to anything less would let the flimsy fig leaf covering slip and show our true fears and failings underneath. We love Christ, but we fear his people.

Christ sacrificed his life to redeem both our relationships with God and our relationships with one another. Because we no longer have to hide from God in our sin, we don't have to hide from his people either. Christ did not save us to be "an only child"[1] in our faith—struggling on our own to fulfill God's kingdom purposes. Instead, he adopted us into a family of brothers and sisters he is perfecting alongside us. We are designed to work together to fight the lies of this world, remind each other of truth, and live according to God's promises.

---

1. Eugene H. Peterson, *A Long Obedience in the Same Direction: Discipleship in an Instant Society,* 2nd ed. (Downers Grove, IL: InterVarsity Press, 2000), 175.

I know this kind of true Christian community—one that is open, honest, and vulnerable—is easier said than done. I've walked into countless worship centers, Sunday school rooms, and homes surrounded by other Christians yet still feeling alone. I've looked around at everyone's perfect smiles and wondered if I was good enough for such a group. I've worried my story would be too heavy or too insignificant. I've fretted about whether I would know enough or I would be a know-it-all. I've agonized over how much of myself—my doubts, my sins, my suffering—I could share. At times, I've left these gatherings more hopeful and encouraged. Still other times, I've left exhausted and disheartened.

Christian community is messy. It's scary. It's imperfect. And in our individualistic culture, it's often something we ignore or outright reject. However, Christ's gift of his body is not an ancillary blessing we can take or leave. God prescribed the church to be an indispensable part of our Christian journey. Just as he didn't create man to be alone; we are not saved to be alone. "Our relationship with God is never less than an intimate relationship with Christ, but it is always more than that.... It is impossible to have a relationship with Christ outside of the vital relationship with the church."[2]

---

2. Tish Harrison Warren, *Liturgy of the Ordinary: Sacred Practices in Everyday Life* (Downers Grove, IL: InterVarsity Press, 2019), 118.

We cannot fully experience the love of Christ without experiencing the love of his body. It is one of the greatest gifts Jesus left us—a gift we are commanded to never neglect. It's a gift we shouldn't forsake when it fails us. Instead, we can learn to cultivate the church into the beauty for which it was designed.

When we know Christ is at work perfecting each of us, we can set aside our fig leaves and allow our Christian sisters and brothers to see all our imperfections. "We're perpetually safe to share ourselves with others because we're hidden in God's love forever."[3] Because our satisfaction and sufficiency are secure in Christ, we no longer must fear the judgment of man—especially within the body of Christ.

We are free to release the burden to make ourselves good enough before God and before others and to wholly enter into biblical community, naked and unashamed.

Finding Biblical Community

Several years after my suitemate stood in my doorway and invited me to open my heart, a new friend opened her front door and invited me into authentic community. I stepped into her apartment and took a seat on the couch next to other newlywed women. We were all in the same Sunday school class

---

3. Christine Hoover, *Messy Beautiful Friendship: Finding and Nurturing Deep and Lasting Relationships* (Grand Rapids, MI: Baker Books, 2017), 103.

at church, but most of us didn't know each other outside of a once-a-week gathering. We were students and teachers, nurses and nannies—all joined together on a Saturday morning for coffee, cinnamon rolls, and prayer.

Our host asked us to go around, one by one, and share how we needed prayer. I had prepared my list beforehand. An acceptable number of "needs" that would allow me to participate without giving away the storm brewing in my heart.

Yet I was struck dumb as woman after woman opened up like I had never known before. They confessed sin, shame, and suffering I had rarely heard others speak aloud. As all eyes turned to me, I knew I had a choice—the same choice I had so many years before. Would I be honest with these new friends, these precious sisters in Christ? Would I allow them to be the agents of God's grace in my life? Would I risk letting them know all my imperfections?

I opened my mouth and told them the truth. I confessed my anger and bitterness toward my new husband. I shared the doubts I had about my faith. I told them my worries about my future career. I expressed my longing to know that I was truly enough, that I was accepted by God and his people. All the things I couldn't share years before now fell out of my lips and off my shoulders.

They received my confession with hugs, tissues, and earnest prayer. They bore my burdens, showed me grace, and encouraged me toward faithfulness. They accepted me—imperfections and all.

I treasured those Saturday mornings overflowing with prayer and coffee. Because I was no longer weighed down by expectations to appear perfect, I could open myself to true biblical community with vulnerability and grace. "Vulnerability happens when we trust others with the sensitive areas of our lives, those aspects about us that feel fragile or reveal our imperfections."[4]

When we don't hide behind our self-sufficient striving or our self-condemning shame, we can fully devote ourselves to gathering together and encouraging one another within the body of Christ.

Devoted to One Another

Thus far in Hebrews 10, the author has reminded the church about the sufficiency of Christ in their lives. He's invited them to draw near to God "in full assurance of faith," to "hold on to the confession of our hope," and to encourage one another in "love and good works" (Heb. 10:22–24). Now, he ends this section with a final "let us" exhortation, a reminder that Christ's perfect work in his people is both personal and corporate: "*Let us* consider one another . . . , not neglecting to gather together, as

---

4. Hoover, *Messy Beautiful Friendship*, 80.

some are in the habit of doing, but encouraging each other, and all the more as you see the day approaching" (Heb. 10:24–25, emphasis added).

This verse applies to more than just regular church attendance. We can see this kind of biblical community fostered in the early church: "Every day they devoted themselves to meeting together in the temple, and broke bread from house to house. They ate their food with joyful and sincere hearts, praising God and enjoying the favor of all the people" (Acts 2:46–47). Biblical community is more than hearing truth from a preacher once a week. It's speaking the Word of God to one another throughout the week. It's more than a few corporate prayers and hymns. It's consistently interceding for each other and praising God for his faithfulness to one another. It's more than a weekly gathering. It's regularly joining together and encouraging each other—whether in person or in spirit—until we all reach eternity.

The early church gave their very lives to cultivate biblical community because they knew their new life in Christ could not survive apart from his body. Likewise, are we willing to devote our lives to the same kind of biblical community?

Scripture has a lot to say about how believers are to devote ourselves to one another every day. Paul reminds the church at Rome to "take the lead in honoring one another" (Rom. 12:10) and to "live in harmony with one another" (v. 16). To the Galatian church he wrote: "Serve one another through love" (Gal. 5:13), and "carry one another's burdens" (6:2). To the church at Ephesus he instructed: "Be kind and compassionate to one another, forgiving one another, just as God also forgave you in Christ" (Eph. 4:32).

This is only a fraction of the instruction God has given us for how we are to treat one another, especially within the church. Jesus summarizes these "one anothers" in a single commandment: "Love one another. Just as I have loved you, you are also to love one another" (John 13:34). Jesus's faithful love for us was never supposed to terminate with you or me. When we are filled with Jesus's love, it overflows to those around us. After we experience God's faithful love, forbearance, grace, and compassion, we then show it to one another. "God Himself taught us to meet one another as God has met us in Christ."[5] This kind of unconditional love would be the primary marker of the people of God. "By this everyone will know that you are my disciples, if you love one another" (v. 35).

So how do we fulfill Jesus's command to love one another? How do we practice biblical community which displays a faithful love the world has never before seen? While we will spend our lives learning how best to minister to others within the

---

5. Dietrich Bonhoeffer, *Life Together* (New York: Harper & Row Publishers, Inc., 1954), 25.

church, we can begin by confessing our sins to others, serving each other in trials, and exhorting one another to faithfulness.

Confession

I remember the first time I confessed my sin to someone when I was twenty-one years old. Of course, I had frequently confessed what I thought were "little" or "acceptable" sins. But the deepest sin struggles I kept hidden for years until they threatened to pull me under. I sat with my small group leader, Ashley, at lunch—unable to touch my salad because of the butterflies warring in my stomach.

Ashley finally asked why I wanted to meet. I kept my eyes down, took a deep breath, and let the words flow out as fast as they could. I waited for the shock, the surprise that a "good Christian girl" would struggle with something like this. I waited for the admonition that I needed to step back from serving in the church lest my imperfections infect others. I waited for the judgment I was sure I deserved.

It never came.

To my surprise, Ashley reached out, took my hand, and responded with grace and gentleness. She reassured me that I was not the only one. I was still loved by God and by her despite my sin. She also responded with encouragement and practical ways to fight this temptation. We dug into the root of my sin, discussed truths to fight the lies, and set up means for accountability.

I left our lunch meeting with a sense of freedom I hadn't experienced before. I felt released from the shame of concealed sin and also empowered to fight the temptation with Ashley beside me.

One of the most powerful duties Christ gave his body was the ability to confess our sins to one another and receive his grace and exhortation. James instructs us: "Confess your sins to one another and pray for one another, so that you may be healed" (James 5:16). We will always find forgiveness when we confess our sins to God. However, he has prescribed that we will only find full healing when we also confess our sins to one another in biblical community. Even though this honesty often comes with the risk of further hurt, rather than healing.

Without the vulnerability of confession, we cannot build true Christian fellowship because we are not being our full selves. "The sin concealed separated the sinner from the fellowship, . . . the sin confessed has helped him to find true fellowship within the brethren in Jesus Christ."[6] As we confess our sins within the body of Christ, we are freed from our shame and strengthened for obedience.

---

6. Bonhoeffer, *Life Together*, 113.

Service

My husband and I got the call at 10:57 a.m. that a two-month-old baby girl in a local hospital NICU would be ours. With tears of joy streaming down my face, I spun into a flurry of activity—packing bags, finding baby clothes, and securing childcare for our older two children. Within two hours, we would be at the hospital to sign the adoption papers and begin a new stage for our family. Looking back, we could not have made it through that whirlwind of a season without the help of our local church body.

Our van wouldn't start on the way to the hospital, and a man from our small group came over and installed a new battery. A group of older women in our church went from store to store, searching for my daughter's specialty formula during the formula shortage. "Text me where you keep your cleaning supplies," a mentor messaged me. "I'm coming over to clean your house before you come home."

At first, it was humbling to have someone meet our most basic needs—even cleaning our bathrooms. In my pride, I would much rather be the one serving others. I would rather be the one listening to someone who is struggling than admit I am struggling. I would rather bring the casserole to your house than ask for help to put dinner on our table. While Christ called us to be servants, our acts of service are often done out of our self-sufficient pride instead of Christ's humility. We feel we must always be the one to serve, because to ask others for help means we are not sufficient in ourselves.

When we understand that our sufficiency is secure in Christ, we are freed to allow others to meet our needs. Christ has given each of us different gifts, ministries, and activities so we can serve one another.[7] God has designed us to be unique yet unified, "so that there would be no division in the body, but that the members would have the same concern for each other" (1 Cor. 12:25). In the same way we can use our strengths to help others in their weaknesses, we can turn to others for strength in our weakness.

We often wish Jesus was here in the flesh working miracles of healing and provision. Yet we sometimes deny his means of miraculous provision in our life by refusing the help of his hands and feet—the church. In biblical community, Christ has called us to humble ourselves both in how we serve others *and* in how we are served by others.

Exhortation

By lunchtime on Saturday, I wasn't sure I would make it through the weekend as sickness swept through my household. What was supposed to have been a relaxing day by myself to

---

7. 1 Corinthians 12:4–7

write turned into a constant rotation of doling out medicines, turning on Disney movies, and brewing more coffee.

In a moment of desperation, I pulled out my phone and texted my friend Rachael. I furiously typed out every frustration and discouragement. I confessed to her my bitterness toward my husband who couldn't help because he, too, was sick. My anger toward God who didn't let things go according to my plans. The guilt at not serving my family with joy.

Though Rachael has her own busy life with as many kids and as full of a schedule, she texted me back soon after. When I clicked open her message, I found my dear friend didn't offer a pithy encouragement of "You've got this!" Neither did she affirm my self-pitying rant. Instead, she pointed me to the truth that my time is in God's hands.[8] She reminded me that even hard weekends like this are in God's control. She texted me a prayer and checked in on me later that day. More than simple words of affirmation, my friend Rachael encouraged me to fight the lies I was believing with God's truth so I could walk forward in obedience.

When the author of Hebrews commanded believers to encourage one another, he knew we are forgetful people. We often need brothers and sisters in Christ to remind us of the truths about who God is, who we are, and how he is at work

---

8. Psalm 31:15 ESV

inside of us. Earlier in his sermon, the writer called believers to "exhort one another every day, as long as it is called 'today,' that none of you may be hardened by the deceitfulness of sin" (Heb. 3:13 ESV). The Greek word translated "exhort" in this verse means to come alongside—to console, to encourage, to strengthen, to comfort.[9] We cannot fully grow in Christlikeness without the help of our brothers and sisters in Christ.

We know God designed our spiritual growth to be empowered by his Spirit inside of us (as we saw in the last chapter). But God has also ordained that our spiritual growth be fueled by his body, the church, around us. Our intentional and vulnerable relationships with other believers are a crucial means of God's grace in our lives.

None of these practices are possible if we don't open our lives to the body of Christ. We can't receive forgiveness if we don't confess our sins. We can't be served if we don't express our needs. We can't be encouraged with truth if we don't share our doubts. Biblical community is only possible if we open up our lives to others—and oftentimes it requires us to take the risk of going first.

---

9. John Strong, "parakaleō," *Strong's Greek Lexicon (KJV)*, Blue Letter Bible, accessed February 8, 2024, https://www.blueletterbible.org/lexicon/g3870/kjv/tr/0-1/.

The Unfortunate Reality of "Church Hurt"

I've shared some beautiful stories of Christian community in this chapter—how Christian sisters and brothers have made space for me to confess my sins, ask for help, and walk in obedience. Nonetheless, I'm not so naïve as to think it's always this way.

Sometimes within the church, our confession of sin is met with judgment and condemnation. Sometimes our needs are met with indifference or rejection. Sometimes our burdens are ignored or insulted. "Church hurt" is real. People within the church use the vulnerability of others to manipulate, abuse, and demean. Although the church is the body of Christ, it is not always Christ-like in its actions.

There may be times when you need to step away from a specific church family because they have injured you. There may be seasons when going to a church service seems terrifying and impossible. There may be moments when you wonder if you should give up on biblical community altogether.

Jesus Christ, the Man of Sorrows, is well acquainted with your grief because of his church.[10] He sees every instance of abuse, manipulation, and rejection. When he addressed the churches in the book of Revelation, Jesus called them out for their specific sins: apathy, false doctrine, immorality, and dead

---

10. Isaiah 53:3

works.[11] Though these faith communities looked pristine on the outside, he knew the darkness on the inside. Despite the failings of his church, Jesus still pursued her, called her to repentance, and covered her with his righteousness. While Jesus is perfecting you, he is also perfecting his whole church.

As Christ heals you from your wounds inflicted by his own people, I pray he would also provide you with fresh hope for his bride. I pray he would give you a vision for what his people will one day be in him. Christ loved his church so much, he "gave himself for her to make her holy, cleansing her with the washing of water by the word. He did this to present the church to himself in splendor, without spot or wrinkle or anything like that, but holy and blameless" (Eph. 5:25–27).

When we experience church hurt, we can look forward to the day when Jesus the bridegroom returns for his bride. He will take all her sin and sorrow, and he will adorn her with his light and purity.[12] We, as part of his body, will enjoy perfect and pure unity with both our God and with his people forever.

Perfected Together

I know what it's like to finish reading a book, feeling convicted to grow in my knowledge, my faith, and my obedience.

---

11. Revelation 2–3
12. Revelation 19:7–8

Yet no matter how good the book is, it often gets put back on my shelf and I'm left remembering only fleeting remnants from its pages.

I've found, however, that the volumes I read in book clubs are different. Those books stick with me longer because I explored their contents with others. I could tell you stories of the coffee shops, the living room couches, and the Zoom meetings where a truth from a book broke through my heart. We are more transformed by truth when we learn within community.

As we are drawing near to the close of this book, I hope you won't keep the truths and promises you've learned to yourself. Invite your friend, your neighbor, your sister, your mother, or your daughter into this journey alongside you.

As you continue to battle self-righteousness, self-condemnation, and self-sufficiency, you will need the antidote to "self." You will need a biblical community where you can speak the lies festering in your heart and be reminded of God's truth. "God has willed that we should seek and find His living Word in the witness of a brother [and a sister], in the mouth of man. Therefore, the Christian needs another Christian who speaks God's Word to him."[13] You are not meant to fight this battle alone.

---

13. Bonhoeffer, *Life Together*, 23.

Friend, I pray you would be so secure in God's love for you that you're willing to be open, honest, and vulnerable with his people. I pray when you walk into a gathering of believers, you're not worried about the way you look, how late you are, or how much you've messed up. I pray you would be able to answer truthfully when someone asks, "How are you?" I pray you would be able to remove the fig leaves of your shame and striving and let the body of Christ see who you really are. I pray that if you don't see this happening within your own local church, you would be willing to go first—to open your front door, your heart, and your life to the body of Christ. I pray you would find true wholeness in Christ as an integral part of his body.

May you find the full freedom of Christ within his church as you gather together. May you encourage one another to fight the lies with God's truths so you can live in light of his promises.

 ## Remember

When you feel alone in your struggles, you can trade your shame and striving for the truth that:

I am enough because I am a part of Christ's body.

Reflect

1. In the past, have you tried to hide your true self from the local church? If so, why have you struggled to trust Christ's body?

2. Which of the three ways we can be devoted to one another—confession, service, and exhortation—do you need to pursue? Write down a way you can practice one of these within your local body this week.

3. Have you shared your struggle with shame and striving with anyone? Identify one person within your local church with whom you can share the truths you are learning from this book (and other truths you are learning!).

Read

For further study, read 1 Corinthians 13. While this passage is often used to describe marital love, Paul originally wrote it to encourage genuine love within the church. Praise Christ for how he is the perfect embodiment of this kind of love. Pray that God would grow this kind of love within your local church, and that he would strengthen you to go first.

Conclusion

I struggled with perfectionism every day while writing this book. With each word I typed, I could hear Satan whispering in my ear, "You have no right to write this book. You yelled at your kids on the way to your office. You spent more time looking at your phone this morning than reading God's Word. You still trust in your own strivings, so how can you teach others to rest in the finished work of Christ?" The accusations rang out louder than my keystrokes—*you are not enough.*

One afternoon while working on my manuscript, I sat frozen before the computer screen. I would write one sentence, then delete the previous three. Fear and shame reverberated in my heart. Doubts clouded my mind. I wondered if I should close my laptop, cancel my contract, and pretend like this never happened.

My head fell into my hands, and tears fell onto my desk. I pleaded with God, *Why would you call me to write this book if I couldn't finish it? Why do I feel like I'm failing in every aspect of my life right now? Will I ever feel like I'm enough?*

While I continued to pray and weep, the Holy Spirit spoke softly to me. He reminded me that I was believing lies. I was forgetting the very truths I spent hours writing about. I wasn't living according to the promise of Christ's perfected work in and through me. The Spirit pointed me to the hope of God's Word: "He who started a good work in you will carry it on to completion until the day of Christ Jesus" (Phil. 1:6). The God who began good work in me—writing a book, serving in my church, loving my family, and so much more—the same God would carry me through to the end.

I need the message of this book just as much as you do. I have to consistently fight the lies with the truth so that I can walk in the freedom of God's promises. And, friend, the good news is that this same freedom is available to you too.

If you've reached this point and are wondering to yourself, *I only wish I could experience freedom like that, but I'm too far gone. I can't control my anxiety. I can't let go of my shame. I can't set down these burdensome expectations. God can't love me unconditionally like that. There's no way I could ever experience true wholeness.* Dear sister, do not let Satan keep you in the darkness of his deceit. You don't have to live in your self-sufficiency and self-condemnation any longer.

It's time for us to fight back and choose to walk in the light.

This Means War

While your everyday life may seem like an ordinary rotation of emails and deadlines, dishes and laundry, conversations and commutes—there is a supernatural war waging around you. Your struggle with shame and striving may appear to only be a battle in your mind and heart, but it is actually spiritual warfare. Paul warns us: "For our struggle is not against flesh and blood, but against the rulers, against the authorities, against the cosmic powers of this darkness, against evil, spiritual forces in the heavens" (Eph. 6:12). The same serpent that deceived Eve in the garden is actively at work to deceive you and me.

When I hear Satan tell me I'm not enough, that Christ is not enough for me, I must take that thought captive and point myself back to God's truth.[1] Even when my heart doesn't feel like it, I must choose to believe God's promises and walk forward in faith, hope, obedience, and community. When I do this, I am waging war against the cosmic forces of darkness around me. And by the power of Christ in me, he has guaranteed me victory.[2]

He guarantees you that same victory! So, friend, I invite you to link arms with me in this daily battle to identify the lies, meditate on the truth, and live according to the promises of Christ.

---

1. 2 Corinthians 10:5
2. 1 Corinthians 15:57

Identify the Lies

I was graduating with my master's degree in less than a month and had secured my dream job. I sat at my graduate assistant desk, shopping for Loft business casual apparel, when the neighboring undergraduate assistant walked over, beaming with pride. She announced that she, too, had just been offered her dream job—one that was a higher position and pay than mine. Almost instinctively, heat flushed my cheeks and tears threatened my eyes. I congratulated her then turned back to my computer, feeling jealous and embarrassed. The job I had been praising God for only moments before now didn't seem like enough.

I knew my emotions were lying to me, but I didn't know how to redirect them. The Holy Spirit prompted me to pull out a notepad and write down all the thoughts leading me to jealousy and discontentment:

> A certain job title equals success.
>
> People will think I'm a failure if I don't get a high-paying job.
>
> I chose the wrong job—or even worse, God chose the wrong job for me.
>
> Her success means that mine is not enough.

I continued down the sheet, watching the lies which were embedded into my heart fill the page.

When you feel anxiety, shame, or pride threaten to overcome your heart, take a moment to pray and to write down what lies you are believing. Be honest with yourself, even if the falsehoods which surface surprise you. Your heart is prone to deceive you,[3] and the first step to fighting its lies is to expose them.

You cannot live in the freedom of Christ's wholeness if you have not yet admitted the strongholds keeping you in shame and striving.

Meditate on the Truth

I sat back and looked at the list of deceptions festering in my heart. By the Spirit, I prayed and confessed the lies I had believed and asked God to reveal the truths I knew from Scripture. I began at the top of my list, crossing out each lie and replacing it with God's Word:

Faithfulness to God is success in his kingdom.[4]

I work unto the Lord and not unto man.[5]

---

3. Jeremiah 17:9
4. Matthew 6:33
5. Colossians 3:22–24

God's good purpose for my life will prevail.[6]

I am enough because Christ has made me enough in him.[7]

While my emotions still roiled, I had a firm foundation of truth to direct my attitude and actions in response.

When you feel the accuser sneaking in, reminding you of your imperfections, you can fight back with "the sword of the Spirit—which is the word of God" (Eph. 6:17). Rather than lingering in the lies, you can meditate on scriptural truths (maybe even some you read in this book). You can hide them in your heart and keep them in your pocket so you can remind Satan and yourself of who God is, who you are, and what God is doing in you.

After listing the lies you are believing, write down corresponding Scriptures that shine the light of truth. When you're tempted to believe that lie again, turn your eyes and heart back to the inventory of God's truths. Study these verses, memorize them, and preach them over your life.

One by one, we can extinguish the flaming arrows of the enemy by guarding our hearts and minds with God's truth.

---

6. Psalm 138:8
7. 2 Corinthians 3:4–6

Live According to the Promises

It took the rest of the workday and much prayer, but as I left the office, I told my coworker again that I was happy for her—and I knew I meant it this time. The darkness that had crept its way across my heart had been pushed back with the light of truth. With my life founded on God's Word, I felt assured that God knew what was best for me. I had hope in the future he had planned. I could work hard as unto the Lord, even if the pay and prestige was less than others received. And that night, I shared with a friend about the difficult day I had so that she could encourage me as I transitioned to my new job.

Satan will seek to incapacitate you as a follower of Christ at every turn by having you believe lies about yourself rather than the truth of who Christ says you are. Even if you do not yet feel the truths you are preaching to yourself, you can move forward trusting God will be faithful to his promises. David preached to his own soul, reminding himself to live according to the hope of God: "Why, my soul, are you so dejected? Why are you in such turmoil? Put your hope in God, for I will still praise him, my Savior and my God" (Ps. 42:5). When we fight the lies with truth, we can walk forward in assurance of faith, enduring hope, love-motivated good works, and biblical community even when our soul doesn't feel like it.

Fighting the lies with truth is not a one-time decision. This process takes discipline. It takes practice. It's a daily "renewing of your mind" (Rom. 12:2)—an everyday battle to align your life with what is true. But you are not alone on this journey. With the Spirit of Christ in you and the body of Christ around you, you can trade your shame and striving for wholeness in Christ.

The empty flatteries of this world can never ward off the deceptive attacks of Satan. Instead, friend, you can rest secure in the truth that Christ has perfected you forever.

Perfected Forever

I opened this book with the question I've often asked myself: "Am I good enough?" I've often felt I was being honest—humble even—when I admitted I wasn't enough. Yet in light of the gospel truth we've learned from Hebrews 10, I realize now those feelings of insufficiency were never accurate. Welsh minister Martyn Lloyd-Jones wrote:

> "I am not good enough." It sounds very modest, but it is the lie of the devil, it is a denial of the faith. You think that you are being humble. But you will never be good enough; nobody has ever been good enough. The essence of the Christian salvation is to say that "He is good enough and that I am in Him!"[8]

---

8. D. Martyn Lloyd-Jones, *Spiritual Depression: Its Causes and Cure* (Grand Rapids: Eerdmans, 1965), 34.

We are wholly satisfied and sufficient because we are in Christ. That is the hope of the gospel that we need to be reminded of every day.

God knew there was nothing you could do on your own to make yourself good enough. He grieved as his people swung between self-condemning shame and self-sufficient striving. So God the Son came to dwell with us in the flesh—fully God and fully man. In his divinity, Christ Jesus perfectly displayed God's faithful love, compassion, grace, and patience toward us. In his humanity, Jesus humbled himself to sympathize with our weakness and limits. He demonstrated the dignity of God's image-bearers and fulfilled the good work the Father prepared for him.

When Jesus hung from the cross, one of his final sentences was, "It is finished" (John 19:30). The Greek word for "finished"[9] in this verse comes from the same root as the word *perfected*[10] we read in Hebrews 10:14: "For by one offering he has perfected forever those who are sanctified." When Jesus offered his life as the final sacrifice, he paid the price for our sin and reconciled us to the Father. When we repent and believe in him, Jesus fully covers us in his righteousness. Moreover, Jesus continues to transform us from the inside out to make us perfect like him.

---

9. James Strong, "teleō," *Strong's Greek Lexicon (KJV)*, Blue Letter Bible, accessed February 22, 2024, https://www.blueletterbible.org/lexicon/g5055/kjv/tr/0-1/.
10. Strong, "teleioō," Blue Letter Bible, *Strong's Greek Lexicon (KJV)*, accessed February 22, 2024, https://www.blueletterbible.org/lexicon/g5048/kjv/tr/0-1/.

More than two thousand years before we were even born, Christ had already accomplished everything needed to make his people enough. Through his death, Jesus perfected us forever.

> Even when you keep making the same mistakes, Christ has perfected you forever.

> Even when you fail to reach your ambitious goals, Christ has perfected you forever.

> Even when others are disappointed in you, Christ has perfected you forever.

> Even when you can't hold everything together, Christ has perfected you forever.

> Even when you're stuck in your shame and striving, Christ has perfected you forever.

Friend, will you lift your gaze from yourself—from your fears and failures—and look to Jesus Christ, seated at the right hand of God? Because Jesus is our perfect sacrifice, we can have assurance of faith to draw near to God. Because he has secured our future, we can have enduring hope in suffering. Because he sent the Holy Spirit to empower us, our good works overflow out of love. Because he has made us members of his body, we can be encouraged by biblical community. We are enough in him.

More Than Enough

As we saw in chapter 5, we will not enjoy all the benefits of Christ's perfecting work outside of heaven. The battle to fight the lies with the truth will never be finished until we reach eternity. That may seem discouraging, but we know how the story will end. As one of my favorite songs proclaims, we are fighting a battle that Christ has already won.[11]

So as we see that day approaching, we fix our eyes on Jesus, who is "the pioneer and perfecter of our faith" (Heb. 12:2). We look forward to when Christ will come again, and we will walk in the fullness of our perfection. Every crack will be mended, every struggle released, every doubt answered. We will finally and fully be whole in Christ. Until then we cry out with the saints, "Come, Lord Jesus!" (Rev. 22:20).

As you finish this book, I pray you now know your satisfaction and sufficiency is found in Christ alone. I pray you can release your shame from imperfections and your striving for perfection. I pray you would discover true wholeness in Christ. I pray you would set your mind on these truths, believe them in your heart, and walk in obedience to them. More than anything, I pray that the next time you wonder if you are good enough, you will hold fast to a better truth:

I am perfected in Christ.

---

11. Shane & Shane, "You've Already Won," Track 2 on *Psalms, Hymns, and Spiritual Songs (Live)*, The Worship Initiative, 2023.